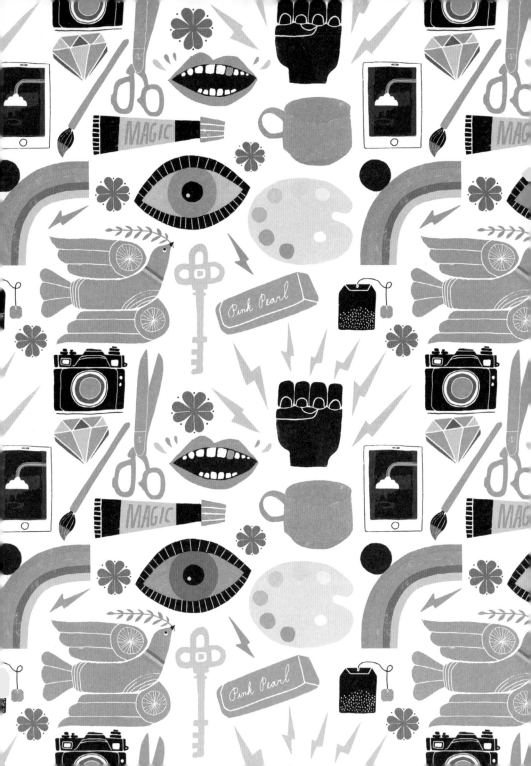

FIND YOUR ARTISTIC VOICE

FIND YOUR ARTISTIC VOICE

THE ESSENTIAL GUIDE TO WORKING YOUR CREATIVE MAGIC

By Lisa Congdon

CHRONICLE BOOKS

SAN FRANCISCO

For my wife, Clay Lauren Walsh,
who is by my side with her heart wide open
every single day on this journey.

Library of Congress Cataloging-in-Publication Data available.

ISBN: 978-1-4521-6886-9

Manufactured in China.

Design by Kristen Hewitt.

10 9 8 7

Chronicle books and gifts are available at special quantity
discounts to corporations, professional associations, literacy
programs, and other organizations. For details and discount
information, please contact our premiums department at
corporatesales@chroniclebooks.com or at 1-800-759-0190.

Chronicle Books LLC
680 Second Street
San Francisco, California 94107
www.chroniclebooks.com

CONTENTS

CONFORMITY IS FOR THE BIRDS

Nonconformity is not only a desirable thing, it is a fac-tual thing . . . all art is based on nonconformity . . . With-out nonconformity, we would have had no Bill of Rights or Magna Carta, no public education system, no nation upon this continent, no continent, no science at all, no philosophy, and considerably fewer religions.

—Ben Shahn

When I was a kid, I wanted nothing more than to fit in. I grew up in the 1970s and '80s in suburban Northern California, in a neighborhood of cookie-cutter tract homes—ours was exactly the same as about twelve others on the street. On the first day of sixth grade, Lisa Bundy, my assigned desk mate, turned to me and asked where my mom bought my clothes. "JCPenney?" I replied sheep-ishly. "Oh, no," she said with disdain. "Bullock's is the best place to buy clothes. JCPenney is tacky." I went home that day and informed my mother in no uncer-tain terms that I was only shopping at Bullock's from that day forward. In junior high and high school, I studied with devotion the then-popular *Official Preppy Handbook*, the ultimate guidebook for conforming. Years later, I went off to a Catholic college, and despite the fact that I was not Catholic or at all religious,

I began attending Catholic Mass with my friends, simply so that I would feel more accepted and part of the crowd. For the first part of my life, conformity was everything to me. I just wanted to be like everyone else.

When I was twenty-two years old, in May of 1990, I graduated from that Catholic college and moved the next day, quite fortuitously, to the city of San Francisco, and my entire interior world exploded. I realized after only a week there what Ben Shahn once so eloquently expressed: Conformity was for the birds. For the first time in my life, I was surrounded by diverse cultures, a spectrum of gender identities and sexual orientations, books, film, and fashion—and, most significantly, *art*.

I became a voracious consumer of art—in particular, visual art—and I began visiting museums whenever I could, borrowing books about art and design movements from the library, or purchasing used copies of artists' biographies at my local bookshop and reading them with devotion. Through this new window into the world, I began to appreciate the value in being different and in putting one's own ideas—however weird they might be—into the world. From there, the pendulum began to swing in the other direction. Each day that passed, I began more and more to value nonconformity, not only in others, but also in myself.

But it wasn't until I began making art (inspired, in part, by all the artists I was reading about) and began to identify as an artist myself that I appreciated how profoundly important nonconformity was. While in mainstream culture, idiosyncrasies and differences are often seen as flaws; in our world—the world of artists—they are your *strength*. They are part of what embody your artistic "voice": all of the characteristics that make your artwork distinct from the artwork of other artists, like how you use colors or symbols, how you apply lines and patterns, your subject matter choices, and what your work communicates.

Like most people, deep down inside, I have always felt a tension between fitting in and standing out. When I began making art in my early thirties as a hobby, and then again when I began my professional career nearly a decade later,

I found myself pondering endless questions about where I was headed as an artist. "Do I want to become part of a movement in art or a particular genre? Do I want to focus on or ignore what is currently trendy? Is it even possible to be completely original? Who do I want to be as an artist? What do I want to communicate through my work?"

What I didn't fully understand at the time was that asking these kinds of questions was an indicator that I was in the beginning stages of discovering (and working toward) my own artistic voice—all the specific stories, colors, markers, symbols, lines, and patterns that I would eventually infuse into my work. When we are in the process of finding our artistic voice, we are almost constantly straddling the planes of belonging and independence, of being part of a movement and having our own unique form of expression, of emulating artists we admire and breaking away from them.

Finding your voice is one of the most important experiences you will ever have. And the process cannot be rushed. Likewise, it isn't just something that magically "happens." Instead, it's both an exercise in discipline and a process of discovery that allows for—and requires—a lot of experimentation and failure. Most of the time, finding your voice takes years of practice and repetition, frustration, agony, humiliation, and self-doubt.

Given its importance, and the challenges associated with it, you'd think the process of developing your artistic voice is something artists would talk about openly, all the time. And yet it is a topic we rarely discuss, except perhaps in some art education programs. The truth is, there are very few artists out there, especially in the first years of their treks, who haven't wondered at some point or another, "Have I found my voice yet?" Or, most certainly, "When will I finally find my voice?" Or "I think I've found it, but how can I be sure?"

These questions are common because the process of finding your voice can feel mysterious or daunting, like something only "certain other" people are born with the ability to achieve. Contributing to the mystery is the fact that there is no absolute, clear, and perfectly defined, measurable picture of what finding your voice looks like. In fact, every artist's voice looks and feels different. By definition, your artistic voice is what *differentiates* you from other artists, *not* what makes you similar. By contrast, for example, many athletes set performance goals that are measurable and easily comparable to other athletes in the same sport based on set standards: number of goals scored, seconds or minutes it takes to complete a specific distance, or distance completed in a specific amount of time. As an artist, your goals are things like nonconformity and difference, neither of which is based on a shared set of measurable outcomes. When you have found your voice, it will look very different than when I have found mine.

To make matters more confusing, the term "finding your voice" is a bit misleading. Finding your voice sounds like arriving at something fixed and final. It implies that once you have found your artistic voice, it will remain unchanged for eternity. In reality, even once you've found it, your artistic voice is always evolving, sometimes subtly and sometimes in more obvious and intentional ways.

And finally, making things even more complicated, while one of your goals is finding a voice that's distinct from other artists, it rarely happens without their influence. With rare exceptions, we become who we become as artists *because* we are influenced by other artists, not despite that fact. No idea is completely original, and being influenced by the work of other creative people and movements is part of the process of finding your voice.

The process of finding your voice is like uncovering your own superpower. Your artistic voice is what sets you apart and, ultimately, what makes your work interesting, distinctive, worthy of discourse, and desired by others. No matter your medium or genre, having your own voice is the holy grail. I aim to help you understand what it means to have an artistic voice and why having one matters. In this book, I also share approaches for navigating through tricky things like influence and fear, along with practical tips for deepening your voice-finding experience. And you won't just hear from me—you'll find real talk and advice from

ten working artists on the topic. Ultimately, my goal is
demystify the voice-finding process so you can more
easily work your creative magic.

This book is intended for every category of artist: am-
ateurs, lifelong hobby artists, aspiring professionals, and current professionals
alike. Whether you are just starting your artistic journey, are right in the middle
of it, or are rejoining after a hiatus, I hope you find this book edifying, encouraging, and motivating.

—Lisa

CHAPTER ONE

WHAT IS AN ARTISTIC VOICE?

SPEAKING YOUR TRUTH

Your artistic voice is your own point of view as an artist. It includes your particular *style*—things like your own color palette, symbols, lines, and markings—your *skill*, your *subject matter*, your *medium*, and the *consistency* with which you use all of these things. It reflects your unique perspective, life experience, identity, and values, and it is a reflection of what matters to you. Ultimately, it's what makes your work *yours*, what sets your work apart, and what makes it different from everyone else's—even from artists whose work is similar. Your voice is formed over time through continuous experimentation and intentional practice, and from following spurts of inspiration and intuition down long paths of development.

Most artists are so busy simply attempting to produce satisfying work or make a living that they forget that, ultimately, they are making work to communicate their own version of the truth. We make work that mirrors our own deeply held ideas about the world. Those ideas are sometimes really simple things like:

Tulips are pretty.

The sunset is the most beautiful moment in the day.

A simple grid is the most visually satisfying image.

And sometimes our ideas are complex and complicated things like:

I am oppressed.

The universe is chaos.

There is light in struggle.

Most of the time the ways in which your truth emerges from your work are somewhere in the middle, between simple and complicated. What you create and how you communicate your truth reflects your personal history, your identity, your ideas, your hopes, your pains, and your obsessions. Making art is an enormously personal experience, no matter your style or subject matter.

Ultimately, as you work to find your voice, all the elements of your voice (style, skill, subject matter, medium, and consistency) become inextricably enmeshed. Your work simply becomes *yours*. In fact, how the elements of your artistic voice play together is what gives your voice a personality.

But when you are in the process of developing your artistic voice, it's helpful to step back and understand what comprises a voice so you can think about what areas you might want to hone further or develop more deeply. In truth, most artists' voices, while hard to tease apart, have several distinct components. For some artists, certain components are their identifying markers more than other components, but all the components make up one's artistic voice.

Get ready to learn about the major elements of artistic voice: style, skill, subject matter, medium, and consistency.

Often, the word *style* is used interchangeably with voice. So it's worth mentioning both of these facts: style is one of the most significant aspects of your voice, *and* your voice is much more than your style, as you will see. Your artistic style is the look and feel of your work. It includes things like how neat and precise your work is or how loose and messy it is. It includes whether you make work that is representational or abstract, the marks you make in your work, and how those marks are repeated.

Here are some examples of things that make up your style. Let's call them the "elements of style":

- **Line.** How do you create lines in your work? Are they delicate and thin or thick and rough? Are they prominent or obscured?

- **Shape.** What shapes do you use consistently in your work? How do you use shape to define your content? Are the shapes in your work geometric or curved? Are the edges soft or hard? Are your shapes flat and one-dimensional or do they have depth and dimension? Are they clean or purposefully messy? Do you render shapes that represent real things or do you use abstract or nonrepresentational shapes?

- **Layering.** Is your work layered? To what extent do you use layers to give the perception of depth and dimension? Or, conversely, is your work intentionally flat and graphic?

- **Color.** What is your typical color palette? Is it warm or cool? What colors are you drawn to? What mood do your color choices give your work? Are you a color minimalist or a color maximalist? Do you play with color values?

- **Texture.** Does your work have texture? How do you create texture with your medium? Or is your work intentionally without texture?

- **Composition.** How do you normally compose your work? Do you consistently use a certain format of canvas, paper, or three-dimensional structure? How do you communicate visual balance? How do you use negative and positive space to impact the overall composition?

- **Rhythm and movement.** How do you convey rhythm and movement in your work? Do you use repetition or alternation of strokes, marks, and imagery, or the gradation of color? Do you create tension by creating opposing directions or with the use of both warm and cool colors? Or, alternatively, is your work purposefully still?

- **Pattern and repeating imagery.** What repeating patterns or repeating imagery do you portray in your work, either within a piece or across pieces?

While most of these elements of style are going to be repeated throughout all of your work, it's also true that you may, like many artists, have more than one style. Some artists make both representational and abstract work. Others make some work that is flat and graphic in style and also work that is more layered and intricate. Having one style is not important. What is important is that you use the elements of style consistently *within* each of your artistic styles. Much more about that in a bit!

SKILL

Skill is an essential element of artistic voice. With greater skill, you'll create richer and more visually complex work, and you'll have a much easier time communicating your ideas or emotions through visual imagery.

Sometimes when we bat around the term "skill," even the most experienced artists will cringe. And that's because for hundreds of years in the art world, until the late nineteenth century, what it meant to be a skilled artist was wrapped up in something very particular: your ability to render something realistically, typically from life. Embedded in that notion of skill were years and years of painstaking practice and academic precision. That old notion is still woven into the fabric of our idea about what it means to have "skill," but it's extremely antiquated.

Thanks to great minds like Georgia O'Keeffe, Claude Monet, Pablo Picasso, Henri Matisse, Sol LeWitt, Romare Bearden, and Vincent van Gogh, by the mid-twentieth century the tradition of a singular definition for artistic "skill" was broken. While most of the artists I mentioned were classically trained, they, along with thousands of others, created works that broke away from the traditional mold of precise representational painting and drawing, and developed now-established genres like impressionism, abstraction, and three-dimensional conceptual works. Each of them forged the way for new styles that broadened our definition of what it means to be a skilled artist. Our growing appreciation of outsider art (art made by untrained artists who live outside mainstream culture) is only a further confirmation of a new definition for artistic skill.

Skill can take many forms, and, according to Dictionary.com, "skill" means "the ability, coming from one's knowledge, practice, aptitude, etc., to do something well." I'll repeat what I think is the most important part of that definition: *to do something well*. Doing something "well" means that you have the technical abilities to execute your ideas in whatever media you use. It also means that you can execute with consistency, not just once, but over and over, because you've practiced . . . a lot. If you are self-taught, you can be just as skilled at making art as someone who has had years and years of schooling. Your skill is simply in what **you do**, and not necessarily in traditional techniques. Of course, having skill doesn't mean you won't ever make bad work or create a disaster. Experimentation and failure are part of the creative process for everyone.

10 STEPS TO BUILDING SKILL

1. BEGIN
2. PRACTICE
3. KEEP SHOWING UP
4. PRACTICE MORE
5. STRETCH YOURSELF
6. PRACTICE
7. PRACTICE
8. NOTE YOUR IMPROVEMENT
9. PRACTICE MORE
10. REPEAT

I'll dive into this in far more depth in Chapter 5, but the way to develop skill is to do the same thing over and over until you are able to do it with some amount of ease. In other words, the way to develop skill is through practice. If you practice something enough, you'll become better at it. Take learning a foreign language as an analogy. When you begin to learn a foreign language, you feel clumsy and it's difficult to find the words you need to convey your thoughts. But as you practice and learn the language (and maybe immerse yourself in a culture that uses the language regularly), you develop fluency, and speaking that second language becomes almost second nature. Developing skill in art-making techniques is similar. As you practice and become better and better in drawing, painting, sculpture, photography, ceramics, or whatever your medium, you develop facility and ease. That fluency supports the development of your voice, because when you have a good handle on skills, you can also focus energy on developing the other components of your voice, like subject matter, color, composition, and style.

SUBJECT MATTER

The very first people I interviewed for this book were husband-and-wife illustrators Sean Qualls and Selina Alko, and I was struck that their immediate personal responses to my question "what is an artist's voice" centered predominantly on subject matter and not on style or skill. That might be because their work is highly narrative; it draws on their life experiences and is focused on their mutual interest in telling stories from history, on civil rights, and about social justice. For some artists, subject matter is the most significant aspect of their voice. To most of us who make even vaguely representational works, it's often the defining marker of our voice. What we choose to make a critical part of our expression of our own truth is what we find beautiful or repulsive, interesting or meaningful.

While most subject matter is externally focused—landscape, narrative scenes, objects, and so on—what we are drawn to rendering is deeply personal and different for every artist. Much of what we are drawn to is based on what we've been exposed to in our lives, what surrounds us, what has influenced us: our education, native country, political affiliation, sexual or gender identity, culture, religion, race, ethnicity, sense of privilege (or lack of). Our choice of subject matter is influenced by our sense of morality, our values, and our ideas about what is right and wrong. It's influenced by what we find beautiful or fascinating or even repulsive.

When you are thinking about specific subject matter, it's as important to consider from where you draw inspiration as how you think about *what* you paint. This is especially true for people who paint from their imagination (and not from specific reference) or who make abstract works. These artists still find inspiration in their exterior worlds, but they process and apply that inspiration differently from people who paint directly from photo reference or life. For example, years ago I became enormously interested in Scandinavian design and folk patterns. I had, at the time, never set foot in Scandinavia, so most of my inspiration was gathered from books or perusing the Internet. I devoured so much inspiration that I eventually created my own imaginary scenes, most of which were in some distant, nameless Nordic land; I drew from the inspiration, but I created my own patterns and landscapes. Abstract or nonobjective artists also process inspiration differently. What inspires their work is often the same stuff that inspires representational artists—landscapes, feelings, or colors. But the way they render their subject matter is not literal.

SEAN QUALLS and SELINA ALKO: On Story, Personal Vocabulary, and Collaboration

It is no wonder that award-winning writer-illustrator Selina Alko now spends her days melding words and mixed-media art to convey stories of hope and inspiration, as well as an alternative viewpoint. Growing up in Vancouver, British Columbia, with a Turkish father who spoke seven languages and taught painting, and a mother who worked in the family's century-old metal recycling business, she was surrounded by the melody of words and stories from different places. That diverse worldview has inspired and fueled her ever since, and it is evident in her books: *The Case for Loving: The Fight for Interracial Marriage*, which she co-created with her husband, Sean Qualls; *Why Am I Me?* by Paige Britt and co-illustrated with Qualls; and *B Is for Brooklyn*, which she wrote and illustrated herself.

Sean Qualls is a Brooklyn-based mixed-media collage artist, children's book author, and illustrator who has illustrated several award-winning books for children. He draws inspiration from an array of influences such as film, television, childhood memories, old buildings, nature, folk art, fairy tales, black memorabilia, outsider art, cave paintings, vintage advertisement graphics, psychology, mythology, history, music, and literature. His recent titles include *Why Am I Me?* and *The Case for Loving*, both of which he co-illustrated with his wife, Selina Alko, and *Grandad Mandela*, written by Zindzi Mandela, which he illustrated on his own. Currently, he is working on his debut as an author-illustrator with *The Music, the People*. In addition to creating books and art, he also DJs on occasion.

Lisa: What is an "artist's voice"?

Selina: Everyone has a story. Your voice includes things you've experienced and that are unique to you: your interests, family, and culture. Your voice is also your medium. For example, I love collage, and it includes all of the objects, paper, and patterns I am drawn to and the way I put them together to make something new.

Sean: An artist's voice is how you see and interpret the world. It's your own unique spin on a given subject, a way of seeing and describing the world filtered through your own lens.

Lisa: What are some things you remember about finding your voice?

Selina: I remember I had to block out the negativity and "noise." I began asking myself: "What am I drawn to? How do I want my work to look?"

What is exciting to me?" There is this way that we compare ourselves to other artists. We say, "Oh, I'm not there yet. And why am I doing this anyway, because I am going to fail." Being an artist can feel so competitive—and that is the "noise" that often clouds our ability to be creative. I had to work hard to not let those thoughts get the best of me. I began listening to what I really liked to do. I really like to paint and collect papers, and I really like putting them together. That excites me. I realized that the magic happens in my own private space, not when I'm focused on what other artists are doing.

Sean: I recall that I realized at some point that I was not good at making a sketch in the traditional way we are taught to make sketches. But then I gave myself permission to use different tools. I could use a photocopier to enlarge and reduce things and manipulate images. And then I discovered collage, but I didn't want it to look like everyone else's collage, so I started painting my own papers. The more I realized that I could make my own rules and that I had something unique to offer, the more my work began to appeal to a greater audience. I wasn't thinking specifically about developing my own style; I was just finding ways to keep my work interesting and enjoyable. Your voice develops as a by-product of doing the stuff you enjoy over and over again and making discoveries. Once I dug into what I was obsessed with making, my voice as an artist began to take on a life of its own.

Lisa: You both work by yourselves and also together. What is it like to collaborate with two different voices?

Sean: We evolved together as artists. We have always been out in the world together looking at art. And it turns out that we both like a lot of the same things. Art is one of the most significant things in our connective tissue. So when we started working together, it was a continuation of the conversation we'd been having for years. And what makes it easy is that we are both confident enough in our own voices and our own work from years of working separately, and we are not afraid of being overpowered by the other person.

Selina: We can also help each other when we are stuck. For example, we might have five pieces going for a book, and they're all at different stages. If either one of us has gotten to the point where we don't know what to do next, we can just hand it off to the other person. We trust that the other person will make the piece better and solve problems.

Lisa: You've begun saying that together you've formed a "third voice."

Selina: In the beginning you could really tell, "Oh, Sean did this part and Selina did that part." You could really see our distinct voices. But by our third collaborative book, things became more cohesive. And, yes, Sean likes to say the third artist emerged!

Sean: That is a borrowed term from Leo and Diane Dillon. Sure, we've always been in conversation, and collaborating is an extension of that, but by the third book together, our voices gelled in a way that a new voice emerged. It's kind of like when you listen to two people harmonize together; you can hear their two voices, but you can also hear a third voice.

Lisa: What's your advice for illustrators who are trying to develop a voice?

Sean: Remember that you are being hired to be yourself. Whatever your perspective is, whatever your experience is, that's why people hire you. The whole point of illustration is to help people see things differently. You can only do that if you are coming from your own experience.

Selina: Take a class or change your environment. Expose yourself to new things. Those are all great ways to get new ideas for how to approach your work.

Sean: Your voice becomes stronger as you develop your vocabulary. To do that you want to get out into the world, watch movies, listen to music and podcasts, read books, see art, look for what speaks to you. Surround yourself with voices that challenge you or that you don't understand, not just other artists who resonate for you or who you want to emulate.

Your artistic medium is another part of your voice. The word "media" is the plural form of the word "medium." Your media are the substances and tools you use to give expression and form to your voice: things like paint, graphite, textiles, ink, paper, wood, clay, and the like. Typically you choose a medium or combination of media because you enjoy working with them and they most effectively express what you are trying to communicate. The media you choose influence your style and the mood in your work.

A medium can be anything. Most artists use what we call "traditional" media like paint, paper, or clay. But many artists use nontraditional media like discarded clothing, chewing gum, or even human hair! New forms of three-dimensional art like assemblage, installation, and performance art are entirely media-driven. In performance art, the artist's own body is the medium.

Even categories of traditional media are diverse. For example, in the world of paint, watercolor, gouache, acrylic, and oil paint are all very different from each other, and artists choose them because of the distinct form they give to their ideas. Similarly, digital drawings often have a distinctly different look and feel from drawings made with a pencil or ink, and vector artwork is distinctive from digital drawings made in pixels on a tablet. Potters use different kinds of clay for different purposes and to portray different effects in their work. Literally every category of art, from painting to ceramics to sculpture to photography to animation to printmaking to drawing (and on and on), uses an array of different media.

What's so great about that is that it means your options are endless. Just like for style, there is no rule that says your voice must include only one medium. Many artists use multiple media in their work. I don't mix media too often, but I do create work in about four different media on a regular basis, including acrylic and gouache paints, ink, and digital drawing on a tablet. Recently I've been painting on wood forms and ceramics. I think all the time about the potential media I might use in the future! Some artists mix

media, and those artists are called mixed-media artists. They use cut paper, ink, paint, graphite, and other media together in different combinations.

Talk to almost any artist and they will tell you that employing different media uses different parts of your brain and keeps things interesting in the occasional monotony of the art-making process. Challenging yourself to develop skill in one medium develops your skill in all media. Discovery of a medium's possibilities (or limitations) happens every time you try something new.

CONSISTENCY

A key component of voice is consistency. Consistency is basically another way of saying that you repeat elements within and among your works: similar subject matter, the same media, and elements of style like color, pattern, lines, and markings. As such, your work is identifiably yours. When you settle in on a set of elements—things like style, subject matter, and medium—you make work that follows a set of unwritten rules: a consistent use of positive and negative space, a consistent color palette, subject matter themes, consistent lines and shapes. Conversely, sticking to a consistent set of rules means you are also *excluding* other things. For example, I rarely use the colors orange or purple in my work. In fact, I typically work in the same seven colors. My more limited palette is one of the ways my work is consistent. The good news is that you don't have to be or do everything as an artist. In fact, focusing on a your own set of "rules" (aka, all the ways you like to work) is part of how you will keep your work consistent.

If you are an artist who works in more than one style, over time you'll develop consistency in each of your styles. Painting great Gerhard Richter works both hyper-realistically and abstractly, and his two bodies of work could hardly be more different from one another. But his works are consistent within each of his styles. All his realistic paintings are clearly his realistic paintings, and all his abstract works are clearly his abstract works.

The consistency in your work is the ultimate expression of your voice. When you find that your work begins to use consistent media and subject matters and has a consistent style over time, this is evidence that your voice is emerging. Does consistency mean you'll never experiment or try new things? Of course not! And you wouldn't want to stop experimenting either. Constantly pushing your work to new places is what will keep your voice evolving and keep your work satisfying and engaging for you and the people who follow your work.

ENTERING YOUR OWN ORBIT

As I mentioned, "finding your voice" is a misleading term because it sounds like arriving at something final. It implies that once you have found your voice, you

have made it to something final that will remain unchanged. But in reality, the voices of all artists continue to change over time, simply by virtue of the fact that when we work consistently, evolution happens. We have new ideas and new inspirations, we develop new skills, and we try new things out of sheer boredom. Sometimes these changes are very subtle, and sometimes they are intentional and quite dramatic.

For that reason, instead of arriving at a final destination, I like to think of finding your voice as entering your own "orbit," where you are floating around in your own circular path, like a planet orbits around its own sun. The sun you orbit around is your aptitude and skill, your ideas, your style, your perspective—all the things that make your voice yours. Your sun's gravity keeps you steady, but you are also not in a fixed place; you are always moving and shifting around inside your orbit. And yet, because your sun has been formed over the course of years, you never lose your true artistic essence, no matter what shifts you make in your work.

ANDREA PIPPINS:
On Speaking Your Truth, Authenticity, and Connecting

Andrea Pippins is an American illustrator, designer, and author whose mission is to create visual stories that inspire and empower people of color. Her work has been featured in O: The Oprah Magazine, Family Circle, Essence, Bustle, and more. She's worked with brands like Free People, Bloomberg, Lincoln Center, and the National Museum of African American History and Culture. Andrea is the author of I Love My Hair, a coloring book celebrating various hairstyles and textures; Becoming Me, a journal for young women in which to color, doodle, and brainstorm; and We Inspire Me, a book about the importance of finding your creative tribe. She is also the illustrator of Young, Gifted, and Black, a celebration of fifty-two iconic black heroes. Andrea is based in Stockholm, Sweden.

Lisa: What is an artist's voice?

Andrea: It's a reflection of who you are. It can be a combination of experiences, your thoughts and interests, beliefs, inspirations, and the stories you want to tell, and it really just all comes together and comes through in the creative process. Ultimately, it synthesizes into—and I put this in air quotes—"artwork." So, depending on what you want to create, all of that comes through in what you produce.

Lisa: Why is having your own voice important?

Andrea: It's so important to share who you are, to tell your truth. Thinking about who you are, what you want to say, and how you want to contribute to the cultural conversation—or not—are really important because only *you* can tell your story through your lens. And when we start to copy or mimic other artists, other people who are creating things that maybe we want to create, it gets muddled, and it's not authentically yours. It's really important for artists to think about what they want to say, what they want to put into the world, what experiences they want their audience to have, and what experiences they want to cultivate.

Lisa: And the world needs to hear those different perspectives!

Andrea: Yes! For example, I tend to focus on black women and girls—it's really important for me to highlight them and to highlight their experiences, because a lot of times these stories or experiences are overlooked. There are a lot of people who may be doing the same thing, but through my lens it comes out in a very special and unique way. So shining a light, shining a voice, *having* a voice is super important as an artist because you're living in your truth.

Lisa: You know, it's so interesting, so many people think about or equate voice with style, but so many of the artists that I've interviewed—including you—don't ever even use that word.

Andrea: Style is a very important element of your voice, but it's not the whole package.

Lisa: You have a distinct style. How did it develop?

Andrea: It was years of building on trial and error, taking on certain projects, doing this thing that worked, and doing this thing that didn't work, and then finding a technique or a tool or a medium that I really liked and then pushing that tool or medium further. It also developed by seeing what either my audience or my clients are drawn to, what was selling, and what examples they pull from my website. All those things helped me build my style.

Lisa: What are the elements of your style?

Andrea: I do think consistency is important, and I use really vibrant colors, which I love. I also love really graphic shapes, and I'm really interested and inspired by textiles, like patterned textiles. There's an artist, Malick Sidibé—he was a photographer. I love his work so, so, so much, and what I'm drawn to is that it's black-and-white photography, portraits of just local people in patterned clothing in front of patterned backgrounds, and, yet, there's something so colorful about the imagery, even though it's black and white. I'm always thinking, "How can I bring that into my work?"

Lisa: When did you realize you wanted to be an artist, and what has your path been since that discovery?

Andrea: I've always been an artist, as far back as I can remember. I was that kid who drew, who loved to color and to tell stories. But a lot of us have heard society or parents or families say, "Oh, you can't make money being an artist, and you don't want to be a starving artist." I was determined to still have a creative career, but I knew that it had to be something that would pay the bills.

Lisa: Like something more "practical," so to speak.

Andrea: Yeah, so I pursued graphic design because I felt like it was a great way to bridge my creative interests and finding a steady-paying job. And it was great. It laid the foundation for me. But it wasn't until 2013 that I really started to feel like maybe I was an artist and not necessarily a graphic designer, or I'm both. There was something else happening here that I felt like I needed to explore.

Lisa: Tell us about that discovery.

Andrea: My voice wasn't necessarily supposed to come through as a graphic designer. It was coming through as this artist, and I wasn't being authentic to myself. I felt I was doing some really great work and having some great experiences as a designer and as a design professor, but I was kind of dying on the inside. In 2013, just before my teaching semester started, I was offered a job as a senior designer in New York City, at a television network. They were going to pay me six figures, and I said, "Oh my gosh, this sounds like it could be really great. I could do this and pay off some student loans and live in New York again." But I also said, "I don't want this job." I said no to the job, and I remember crying and feeling really depressed because I thought, "Well, if I don't want that job, and if I don't necessarily want to teach full time anymore, what is it that I want to do?" That started the exploration. I was journaling and taking time to reflect. And I remember, one day, I wrote in my journal, "I am an artist," and that changed everything. That's when I really started to make some shifts in my life.

Lisa: Then a series of interesting events happened.

Andrea: Yes. Illustrator Leah Goren was teaching a workshop with some MFA students, and I went because I love her work. At the end of her presentation, I introduced myself and said, "Oh, I love what you're doing. I follow your work, blah blah blah." And then that following week, Leah's friend, fellow illustrator Julia Rothman invited me to be part of a Ladies

Drawing Night feature for *Ladies Drawing Night,* a book she cowrote with Leah and Rachael Cole that was coming out that next year. We're sitting there that night, and I'm at the table drawing with them, and an art director at Schwartz & Wade Books said, "Hey, does anyone have any ideas for children's books?" And I was sitting there thinking, "Oh my gosh, that's amazing. I would love to do a children's book, but I have no idea what to share right now." So I kept that in the back of my mind, and a few months later, I sent her an email saying, "Hey, I have some ideas for children's books," and that's how *I Love My Hair* happened. So it was all these little things that were happening—going to the workshop, going to the Ladies Drawing Night event, and then making that connection with the art director—a domino effect of events that led to the work I'm doing today.

Lisa: I love that story because that's what happens when you show up. It's not about having an agenda, it's about the connections you make that lead to new opportunities. Just like you did with Leah, I sometimes force myself to walk up to fellow artists or art directors and say, "Hello, my name is Lisa, and I'm an artist, and I love what you do," and sometimes those initial connections lead to friendships or other professional opportunities.

Andrea: Yes! I have tons of stories of how just showing up at a gallery opening has resulted in a longtime friendship. Those connections are not always professional, but they're about having artist friends who can support you and become part of your tribe and give you feedback and advice.

Lisa: What are your primary influences?

Andrea: It all goes back to being a preteen in the early '90s and coming of age in that decade. That era has really influenced my work. Bill Cosby's terrible actions have tainted *The Cosby Show,* but that show had a huge impact on me in seeing black families, or seeing a black family thrive. And then, on *A Different World,* seeing young black teens or young black people going to college. It was just a time when you had a plethora of

black stories in pop culture, so everything from *South Central* the movie and *Boyz n the Hood* to my favorite movie *Love Jones*, or *Boomerang* with Eddie Murphy. It wasn't just black pop culture; it was just pop culture. And pop culture heavily influences my work. I love doing projects that reflect what's happening now in pop culture, whether it's commentary or highlighting a person who needs to be celebrated. I create what I want to see.
It's important for us to show a reflection of communities or stories that we want to see.

Lisa: Your work has this particular mission. What is the role of activism and social change, in particular for black girls, in your voice as an artist?

Andrea: The written word is powerful. When we hear something, it's powerful. But when you see it? That's the most powerful. We learn by seeing. We learn by watching. So we can say all these wonderful things about diversity and inclusion, but when we look at the television, when we look at ads, when we look at illustrations, they don't reflect reality. And my mission really is to offer a different image, a different story. I focus a lot on women and girls because I am a woman, and young black girls often don't see themselves reflected. That's really important to me. When we see reflections of ourselves, we see what we can do. We see what's possible for us.

Lisa: What do you think artists at the beginning of their paths deal with today that you didn't deal with at the beginning of your career, and what are the advantages of the world that we live in today for artists versus the disadvantages?

Andrea: I think because of social media, young people are exposed to so much art and design. And they begin to compare themselves to the people they follow. Like, "Oh my gosh, this person is doing this and doing that, and I should be doing this." And because of social media, people only see glimpses into someone's art career or process. Because they're not seeing the whole story, they're seeing little clips of what's happening and thinking that "Oh, I just need to do XYZ to make it happen." Sometimes quick success does happen, but that's the exception to the rule. People should remember that it's always about the journey, about taking steps, trying different things, experimenting. Nothing happens overnight. When my book came out, people said, "That happened so fast." But it was literally fifteen years of different jobs, building a portfolio, and having different rejections from different publishers for other book ideas that got me to the point where I could have that book deal happen so quickly.

CHAPTER TWO

WHY DOES HAVING A VOICE MATTER?

YOUR VOICE IS YOUR SUPERPOWER

In her book *The Creative Habit*, Twyla Tharp, world-renowned choreographer and dancer, talks about touring with her dance troupe from New York to Los Angeles. One half of the program that they'll perform once they arrive in Los Angeles will be set to Beethoven's Piano Sonata no. 29. This half of the program they've planned and practiced. The other half of the program, Tharp intentionally leaves a mystery until she arrives. She doesn't plan what music she'll be using or which dancers she'll be working with. She won't even think about the lighting or costumes until she arrives. The large white room will become her motivation to create something brand new. For Tharp, the blank space, and the mystery and the challenge that come with more spontaneous acts of creativity, are exciting.

But without the experience of having choreographed hundreds of dances before, and without years of practice and her finely developed artistic perspective, Tharp could never walk into a white room and, in a short period, choreograph a dance for an audience of paying customers. This is where her artistic voice becomes her superpower. Choreographers have artistic voices just like visual artists do, just like writers and musicians, just like anyone in the act of creating. Tharp's well-honed voice allows her not only to confidently choreograph a dance under pressure—it makes that process exciting and enjoyable, something she chooses to do because it yields something fresh and new.

Your creative voice is your superpower, too. When you have developed your voice, you have the power to create—even under pressure—along with the power to influence others and the range and flexibility to express your own point of view with dexterity.

YOUR VOICE IS YOUR STORY AND YOUR STORY MATTERS

How could you live and have no story to tell?

—Fyodor Dostoevsky

In the end, we all become stories.

—Margaret Atwood

Until I was in my mid-thirties, I didn't think my life mattered much or that I had anything interesting to say; making art changed my relationship to my story. One of the outlets that acts of creativity give us is the opportunity to discover, and then to express, what's inside us. And everyone has something inside to express. To be clear, your story isn't necessarily the linear retelling of your life's path, though it could be. Your story is simply everything about you: what has happened to you, what interests you, what you are passionate for, what you find yourself wanting to read about, and what you find yourself thinking about as your mind wanders. It is also your struggles, your fears, your regrets, your hopes, your dreams, and your aspirations. Your story is your background, your identity, your culture, your ethnic or gender or sexual identity, the color of your skin, and how you've been treated by society, and the privilege or lack of that you've experienced in your lifetime because of all of those factors. Discovering your story requires "raking through your life to figure out what's important to you," says ceramics artist Ayumi Horie.

While we might recognize that we have a story, we might also think our story is boring and that no one would be interested in hearing it. This very fear stops countless people from expressing themselves creatively—a fear of not being interesting enough or impressive or dramatic enough, or a fear that their story is too depressing or dark or even too happy or too colorful. So they ask, "What would be the point in sharing it?" But the truth is that everyone's story matters, including yours. The fact that you might not think your story matters is actually just part of your story! Will everyone relate to your story? Of course not. But by expressing it through your art, you will find people who do. People connect with your work for a variety of reasons: it might bring them comfort or give them hope or strength. It might challenge some of their assumptions or it might simply speak to them visually. The possibilities for connection are endless.

One of the things I learned when I began making art was that there was so much more to my story than I ever realized. In fact, once I started to make art, it was like a floodgate opened. The boring interior life I previously related to was transformed into an inner world so intriguing to me that I couldn't contain it. I remember in the early days of my art-making journey, I was drawing detailed renderings of trees as I sat in my sister's living room. At the time, I was obsessed with drawing trees and even entire forests. I studied their intricate motifs and characteristics and drew hundreds of them. I was incredibly inspired by their detailed forms, and they were an important symbol to me of nature's innate display of balance, energy, and stability. Until I began drawing and painting a year or so earlier, my sister, like most people in my life, had never thought of me as a particularly artistic person. "I wonder," she asked as she watched me draw a bark pattern on the trunk of a tree, "has this always been in you?" I often asked myself the same question. "I'm not sure," I responded. Of course, I realize now, years later, that the germs of all the creative inspiration and expression that was pouring out of me at thirty-six years old had always been there. I simply now had a way to articulate it. The truth is, we're all like that, full of things even when we think we're not. One of the greatest things about making art—and about finding your voice as an artist—is that it gives you a channel to release what's inside of you.

EXAMPLES OF THINGS THAT ARE PART OF YOUR STORY

Loves	Spirituality	Favorite books
Regrets	Truths	Turning points
Heartbreaks	Home	Smells
Obsessions	Childhood	Morals
Friendships	Relationships	Cultural icons
Collections	Aversions	Musical interests
Fashion	Daydreams	Memories
Intuition	Fantasies	Differences
Passions	Symbols	Secrets
Repulsions	Mentors	Travel
Gender identity	Teachers	Lessons
Sexual orientation/ identity	Family	Lies
	Obastacles	Hopes
Culture	Triumphs	Dreams
Ethnicity	Goals	Failures
Race	Schooling	Food
Religion	Favorite colors	Mistakes

FIN LEE: On Heart, Your Interior World, and Identity

Fin Lee (LOSTBOY) is a queer, first-generation, Korean American artist whose work spans identity, connections, community, and desire. Their work exists within many mediums: fashion, murals, illustrations, digital content. They have had the honor of having their drawings appear with Lady Gaga (Grammy Performance, 2016), Planned Parenthood (#iDEFY commercial / Shorty Award), the *New York Times*, Samsung, G-Star RAW, Dr. Martens, Bloomingdale's, Campaign Living, *Bitch* magazine, *Hyphen* magazine, La Dispute, Scout Books, LA Coffee Club, Sakura of America, StyleHaul, Disoriented Comedy, and many more amazing clients. They have also been featured on Design Sponge, Upworthy, and BuzzFeed LGBT. Their work has been exhibited nationally, including at Betti Ono (Solo), Co-Lab Gallery (Solo), Los Angeles County Store (Solo), Giant Robot Store, Booooooom x Herschel Supply, Bitch Media (twentieth anniversary show). They live and work in Los Angeles, and are currently pursuing a career in archiving and library sciences while actively working on illustration.

Lisa: What's in a voice?

Fin: Your artistic voice is not so much style as it is heart. You're the only one that has your voice. No one can take that away from you because no one else is you.

Lisa: As much as you try to get away from yourself, you can't. Your voice always comes through.

Fin: Yes! People use descriptors for my work like "therapeutic" or "self-analysis," because my work is centered on myself. I see that in other people's work too. I feel like people see how interior my work is. I don't really go beyond myself a lot of the time to other subject matter, and I think that's really obvious in the way that I live my life because I'm a total hermit! And that comes through in my work.

Lisa: You make both fine art and commercial work. Because your work is so much your inner world, what's the experience like when you're being asked to illustrate something that's somebody else's concept?

Fin: It depends on the client, because I've had such a broad range. For instance, sometimes clients ask you to do things you'd already do on your personal time. A client will see something you drew on social media and email you to say, "We want to pay you for this, and we want to commercialize your aesthetic." And then there's editorial illustration. I am lucky because the art directors who I've worked with personally know the root of what my work is, and, therefore, they choose me for subject matters that match really well with what I do. Maybe that's more me being fortunate, but you also have the freedom to turn down work that doesn't feel like you.

Lisa: I think most art directors hire people, especially people like you who have a super-distinct style, to be you.

Fin: That's also why I have a paying job outside of being an artist. There are luxuries in that because I feel I can be selective with the assignments I get.

Lisa: What is your work about?

Fin: My work is really about my day-to-day life. It's about the people I interact with, the things that are on the news. I've noticed that even when I don't have the words to say how I'm feeling about how messed up this world is, I can still find a way to communicate it, even if it doesn't say, "This is what I'm feeling." It's important enough for me to release those feelings through my art.

Lisa: It is like therapy for you?

Fin: Oh, one hundred percent. After I finished art college, I had this gap of a few years when most art students either continue making art or don't, and I was really heading down the path of not going to pursue art in any way, shape, or form. I've always dealt with depression, and a few years ago, after this short gap, I started to take antidepressants, and after that I really took my art to another level. I started documenting what was going on in my head because the whole process of getting on this chemical train—and I still am, I've been

50 MG

on two different forms of medication since I started—was a way for me to feel sane. I started sharing personal Instagram posts. That sharing started it all. That experience of expressing myself out of the fog of depression was the root of where my artistic voice emerged.

Lisa: How has your work changed over time?

Fin: During college, I drew a lot of figures. I still draw hands, but I drew hands a lot back then too. It was obsessive. I don't know what it was about hands. So in a sense, I am doing the exact opposite of what I was doing because everything was so figurative. My work has always had a sadness to it. I've come to accept that is part of who I am. I am one hundred percent sure my path to happiness is very, very different from everyone else's, and everyone has their unique way of existing in this world. I have chronic depression, and I have to deal with this ambience of depression throughout my whole life. And I think, because of that being such a strong force in my life, it really has been the glue that puts together all my work from college until now. Even if the subject matter is different, I still use the same line work. I still use the same materials. I still watch the same movies and read the same books that influence my work.

Lisa: What do you struggle with in terms of your voice?

Fin: I sometimes have this over-looming feeling that nothing I do matters, and that's the thing I fight with because I know for a fact that that's untrue, even if that's what I hear being echoed in society. It's a huge mental battle, and your mental health affects your art. There are days when I have to find a reason to draw, and I think, more often than not, there are more reasons not to draw than to draw. I don't have a formula—I don't think anyone really does—and I just end up trying to do it when I feel like I want to, as opposed to feeling like I should have to, because that's when the creative process gets muddy.

Lisa: When you do force yourself to sit down and draw, even when you don't feel like it, do you feel like it's worth it sometimes?

Fin: Yes I do, and, actually, learning about other artists who engage in these disciplined daily projects was inspiring to me and spurred my first daily practice. I read something from Kurt Vonnegut, I don't know the direct quote, but he was mentioning that everyone should just write something, draw something, do something, and then throw it away. Just the act of doing something is kind of healthy. I like to remember that a regular practice isn't about having something to show, but rather the practice itself is important.

Lisa: I love the idea of taking the preciousness out of our work. When you do share your work with the world, what compels you?

Fin: Even though I have a wide range of identities, I know that the core thing that I am meant to do and am destined to do is make art and share that work, so that people know that they're not alone in whatever my work is talking about—feminism or queerness or being Korean or first generation; there are all these things that I know that I wanted to connect with when I was younger, but didn't see myself reflected. The handful of times that people have come up to me and reached out to me and said, "This meant something to me," and cry, all these things . . . I couldn't even imagine anyone reacting that way, let alone having a positive reaction from a drawing I made in five minutes. Something as simple as that can change whatever that person is going through. Knowing that my platform is a place where people can connect with me makes me want to push myself more.

Lisa: What role do you think social media plays now, good or bad, in either helping or not helping artists who are just starting out?

Fin: Being a young artist, you're just going to be impressionable. This is all they know—likes and hashtags and trends. Those things fade, though. They don't stay, and that's why I worry about younger artists who think one style is popular, but then there's going to be another style, and so people's individual voices aren't being built on a foundational level because social media is very superficial. I feel like it's easy to connect with a style, for sure. "Oh, I like this person. I like this person's art." But when you don't know yourself before you look at other people's work, that's where it gets dangerous, and people may be making work that's not exactly coming from inside of them but from what they think other people want to see.

Lisa: If you were giving advice to somebody who was struggling with navigating social media while also trying to find their voice, what would you say?

Fin: I think it's just important to listen to yourself and your body, and if you feel yourself tensing up and feeling anxious and ashamed or guilty when you're looking at someone else's social media account, that's when you need to recognize, "This is unreasonable. I need to take a break from this."

Lisa: Who were some of your early influences and how have you moved through them?

Fin: I went to this art prep school during high school, and a lot of what the teachers introduced me to was my foundation. I looked up to Egon Schiele and Gustav Klimt, Käthe Kollwitz. Then later on, I fell in love with Kiki Smith and Julie Mehretu. In general, it just kept evolving because I kept moving. I kept meeting new people. So in terms of influences, mine are all over the place, and I feel really grateful for that because I feel like I have a wider spectrum of ideas. I've been lucky to see a lot of original work in different places. I think that's pretty important in general, just to expose your mind and your eyes to that kind of stuff. Until recently, I didn't even know about Yayoi Kusama, and when I learned about her, I was just like, "Wow!" I had that moment of kindred spirit.

Lisa: Those constant discoveries when you are curious about art are really wonderful.

Fin: Now that the Internet is more popular and people are sharing things and art is around all the time, I'm still always being influenced. I don't think there's a way to say, "This is where I stopped being influenced and just did my own thing," because our influences will always be a part of who we are.

Lisa: What did it feel like when you realized you had found your voice?

Fin: There were maybe two points where that happened. The first time was when I first began taking antidepressants. I felt so different. It was the most natural and the most effortless making art had been for me. I realized I had a voice, even though I probably had it before, but I felt it for the first time. The second moment was when I designed Lady Gaga's background dancers' costumes. Even though there was art direction, it was my work. It was one hundred percent my work. I felt that. It was also the toughest, and probably will be the toughest assignment I've ever had. It was a very, very quick turnaround, and I didn't know I had it in me, to be honest. You know when people say, "Oh, I could've done that," but then, you don't really know until you're in that situation? And I did it. I worked under intense pressure. I think that was probably the first time I was proud of an artistic endeavor and knew that I had a solid artistic voice.

Lisa: What advice do you have for anyone who says, "I wish that I could get to the place where Fin is, making work regularly and having this distinct style and having Lady Gaga call me," who might feel frustrated or like they're never actually going to get there. What advice do you have for people who want to get to a certain place and don't feel like they're there yet?

Fin: That's hard because part of me wants to say, "Don't compare yourself," but then I would be a hypocrite for saying that! We all compare ourselves to others. All I can say is that you just don't know until you put your foot forward. I've been in situations where I was too afraid to submit for a show or contact this art director or that art director who I really wanted to work with. There are too many opportunities like that that are wasted because we're too afraid of rejection. But from my own experience, you have to go through getting rejected.

Lisa: You have to take risks.

Fin: Yeah, because no one has a golden plate for you. Nobody is going to give you everything you want. Ever. You have to work for it.

YOUR VOICE IS AN ESSENTIAL ELEMENT
FOR PROFESSIONAL SUSTAINABILITY

If you have, or aspire to have, a career as a professional artist, your voice is going to be your very best friend in that endeavor. While having a strong artistic voice alone doesn't ensure professional success (things like your desire and your ability to work hard to promote your work, meet deadlines, and effectively manage your time also matter), your voice is a necessary element toward sustaining your artistic career. It's what sets you apart from other artists, what allows others to connect with your work and to find enough value in it to purchase it or pay you to make more of it. For professional artists, this cycle needs to repeat itself over and over and over. Demand for your work is essential to sustain a career, and a strong voice is an essential element in the formula for sustainability of a professional career. The stronger and more distinct your artistic voice, the more likely you will seize opportunities like gallery shows, grants, residencies, illustration gigs, licensing agreements, and sales of both original art and products.

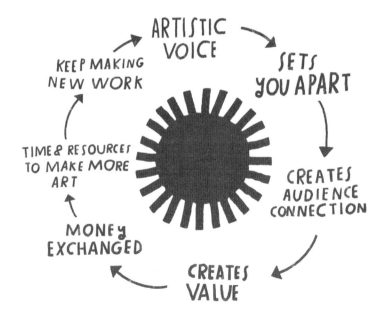

THE DOWNSIDE OF FADS AND TRENDS

Some artists focus heavily on mimicking fads or trends, and doing that might sustain an art practice for a period of time. However, if your work gets stuck in a trend that has been dead for a while or your work changes only when trends shift, it will inevitably fall flat. More importantly, making work that only mimics external market trends will, over time, most likely leave you feeling bored and uninspired. I know this from personal experience. When I was starting out as an illustrator, I was really interested in getting into surface design. I dreamed of having my work on things like wallpaper and fabric. First, I learned how to make repeat patterns, and I practiced by making as many as I could. At the time, I also turned away from my inner well of ideas and began looking at trend reports and saving trendy images on Pinterest as my inspiration. But the problem was that I hadn't fully developed my own voice yet, so referencing industry trends made my work feel boring and humdrum. I was trying to emulate themes and ideas because I thought they might sell, and not because I felt any connection to them or because they were personally interesting to me. Ironically, following trends had the opposite effect on my work than I'd hoped.

One year during this early part of my career, I went to a surface design trade show to exhibit my work at my agent's booth. Buyers from the fashion, home décor, publishing, and stationery industries come to surface design trade shows to license artwork that will adorn everything from clothing to books to pillows to apparel to greeting cards. I remember walking into the giant convention center in New York City and feeling completely overwhelmed. All around me for what seemed like miles were trendy patterns of the current icons of that year: gardening tools, owls, and llamas. I wondered how anyone who was there to purchase designs would ever be able to wade through the mass of sameness. Furthermore, I wondered how could I ever stand out as a surface designer if I was only following subject matter and style trends? Instead of feeling inspired by what I saw, I was wracked with anxiety. That night I got back to my hotel room and cried. I realized that in order to feel excited about my work again, I had to create illustrations based on stuff that was interesting to me (aka *not* gardening tools, owls, and llamas), and I had to make them in a way that felt different and entirely me. I wanted to feel exhilarated by inspiration again.

As an antidote to my anxiety and panic, my partner suggested that I try one of my favorite exercises: brainstorming. The next day, I brainstormed all the stuff that inspired me. And when I got home a few days later, I threw away the trend reports and stopped looking at fads on Pinterest. Instead, I began diving with renewed vigor into subject matter and styles of working that I loved. Of course, some of the stuff I loved was trendy, but I was making decisions based on what spoke to me, not on what I thought I should be making based on the movement of the mass market. Within months, my work shifted significantly. I was having much more fun, and, lo and behold, my career began to take off with new energy. It was also the first period of time I can remember feeling like I was floating around in my own orbit. I was finally finding my voice. As fellow illustrator and designer Carolyn Sewell is famous for saying, "Pleasing everyone is the shortcut to beige." Making only work that you think will please your followers or sell or that follows trends or emulates just one artist isn't just potentially detrimental to the sustainability of your art, it's simply less satisfying. Diving into your own interests and fascinations will not only keep you more engaged in your work, it will also increase the likelihood that your work will stand out as different.

TRUST THE CYCLE

Everyone's artistic path is different, but there are some fairly predictable phases on the path that we all share. The path is never linear or smooth—in fact, it can seem like a bumpy, repetitive cycle. I call the phases: The Spark; The Ongoing Desire to Create; Risk-Taking and Experimentation; Questioning; and Creative Flow. As we cycle through these phases we are sparked with inspiration; we experiment and fail; we push through and achieve something great. Then, inevitably, we bump up against new walls, question our work again, but manage somehow to land in a period of great flow. We cycle through some phases over and over. Understanding where you are in the cycle is useful, because that understanding can help you anticipate where you might be headed next. It can also help you understand that any messiness you are experiencing is completely normal. It can help you to hang in there and persevere, even when you feel like you want to quit.

THE SPARK

If you ask anyone who is on an artistic path to go back to the very first thing or set of things that ignited their interest in making art, they will usually be able to tell you. That's because we all begin our creative journeys with some kind of initial influence. I like to call it a spark. Creativity researchers Scott Barry Kaufman and Carolyn Gregoire refer to it as a "crystallizing moment." For many people, the spark happens when they are a kid or a teenager, and, for others, it doesn't happen until adulthood. For some, it's a book they read or a film they watched or a trip to a museum that changed them forever. For others it's noticing street art on their city block for the first time or feeling mesmerized watching a teacher demonstrate the process of making something. Some people grow up surrounded by art, theater, writing, or music in their families. Others don't discover creativity until much later in life. Your spark is simply a moment or a series of moments that inspired you to want to make art or to become an artist. It's that moment when you first felt a deep connection to some form of art or to the creative process.

Some people act immediately after they experience the initial spark. "I saw this thing that inspired me to want to draw/paint/make/fill-in-the-blank and so I just got the supplies (or improvised) and began." But for many people, the initial spark happens, but it doesn't lead to creative action for many years—or ever. And that's because countless things in life can contribute to stalling or inhibiting active creativity, including family background, messages from parents, insecurity, cultural norms, self-judgment, "shoulds," and "should nots." The messages that art is reserved for only a privileged few, and that it is a useless or even harmful, frivolous activity, are still pervasive in our society. These messages, along with other circumstances and beliefs, lead to countless cases of unexpressed, untapped artistic brilliance.

The good news is, for many of us, the spark does lead to an urge to actually make something, sooner or later. I *want* to paint. I *want* to draw. I *want* to take photographs. I *want* to build something. I *want* to express myself creatively. For some of you, that happened at five years old. For others, it didn't happen until you were sixty-five years old. And when it happened for you doesn't matter. What matters is that you had the urge to make something—to draw, sew, paint, sculpt, photograph, collage, whatever—and you acted on that urge.

After the initial spark happens, it can happen over and over again, often after you make new discoveries that light you up and make you want to go down a different creative path. These sparks are magical, because they make us feel inspired and give us the urge to create.

KINDAH KHALIDY: On Listening to Your Inner Voice and Cultivating Joy

Kindah Khalidy is a California-based painter and textile designer who exhibits fine paintings worldwide. She earned a BFA in painting, drawing, and textiles from California College of the Arts, and she is the author of *Once Upon a Colorful Canvas: A Playful Plan for Learning to Paint*. In addition to her namesake line, Kindah Khalidy, she has collaborated with major apparel brands and companies including Vans, Facebook, Hobes, Land of Nod, Linus Bike, Nordstrom, and Old Navy. She has also partnered with the United Nations and UNICEF on other projects.

Lisa: When did you know you wanted to be an artist?

Kindah: I started my artistic stride early. My mom was always giving my brother and me sketchbooks, markers, pens, and craft supplies when we were little. I never felt scared by them; I always have a really exciting feeling when I begin something. I remember having that feeling as a little kid, and savoring the endless possibilities of a blank piece of paper. I've always had a love for craft supplies—still, when I see glitter, it feels so expensive and luxurious to me. Craft supplies don't really have a specific purpose, so it's up to you to create something with them, and I think I like the mystery about them.

Lisa: Eventually you ventured to art school at California College of the Arts (CCA)?

Kindah: My dad wanted me to get a practical job where I could sustain myself. He really wanted me to become a doctor or go into nursing, so my plan was to go to nursing school. And then, just at the last minute, I put together a portfolio really quickly for art school, and I got in. I remember thinking, "This seems risky, but I've been doing this creative stuff my whole life. I might as well just try." And I got some scholarships, so that helped. I thought I was going to go into fashion, but then I ended up falling in love with a lot of different fine art practices. I ended up doing a program where you can create your own major in the individualized program.

Lisa: You are known for your very whimsical and colorful abstract paintings and textile sculptures. Has your work always been similar?

Kindah: I was talking to a friend who I hadn't seen in a long time and she said, "Your aesthetic hasn't changed at all. You still like confetti and muumuus and shapeless bags." I guess I've been on that track this whole time. Although, my paintings in high school were really, really bad. I tried to draw things I saw around me, like streetlights and other objects. I think I was trying to make something that looked cool, but the technical side wasn't there yet. The content and colors were not very strong either. I can't even look at them now!

Lisa: What happened to the trajectory of your work once you entered CCA?

Kindah: I really fell in love with the hand textile printing classes and all the textile processes and painting. Before I really got into painting and met some great teachers, there was a point where I thought I should drop out of school. You'll hear a lot of people say, "Why go to art school? There's so much you can just discover on your own." I definitely had that moment. But then I stuck in there and ended up meeting really inspiring painting teachers who helped morph my outlook on everything that painting could be. The town I grew up in is kind of famous for its art. They have a lot of little galleries, but very few contemporary galleries. It's mainly ocean landscapes with amazing technical details in oil. I had no real experience with contemporary art until school. Once I learned about the Bay Area art scene, how people were using colors and materials in ways I had never seen, my brain exploded. People were making fine art with glitter and pipe cleaners. It was a dream come true seeing that happen.

From there I made my own major with painting, drawing, textiles, and a little bit of fashion. I could get a little taste of everything. I wanted to learn some technical things in fashion. I wanted to be able to pull an idea out of my head and draw it onto paper. And then I wanted to be able to create my own fabrics, and I knew I'd have to get good at painting to be able to do that.

Lisa: How did your voice develop from there?

Kindah: I started painting abstractly in the way I do now late in my junior year of college. I had this class where we had no instruction. We just went in for six hours and just worked. I find that kind of structureless structure works really well for me. I remember having this moment where I was experimenting with a lot of different materials and different ways of painting, and then something clicked and I realized, "I'm not really enjoying this. What would I enjoy making?" And it just kind of came out, and I've been painting that exact way for eight or nine years.

After school, my paintings grew in the little studio apartment I shared with my boyfriend. And eventually I got a studio outside my home. It was the biggest space I'd ever had, and I really got to make big work in there. I always had this notion in my head like, "I need to be making big work. It's what I really enjoy." So I took the leap and got that space, and that's when things really exploded.

Lisa: How do you approach making a painting?

Kindah: It's very intuitive. I want the process to be very enjoyable, and I don't want to feel guilty or scared to do it. I had to throw a lot of things out the window, and I'm constantly asking myself, "Is this something I enjoy?" Just asking, "Am I excited to go to work? Am I excited about starting something new?" is very important. I think more people should channel that and not be scared to paint. If I tried to paint something like a landscape or something in a certain way, it would be a very unpleasant experience for me. There are a lot of different forms in my work, and it's not so much about creating a certain image or something in my head. I'm having this conversation with myself while I'm working, like, "What would it feel like to put this color next to this one, and how does it feel to make the curves on this shape a certain width around every blob it has?" Just making those conscious decisions as I go, it's just very much a part of the process.

Lisa: It seems like your work is almost meditative, and that you're so present with it that you're actually thinking about how doing something is going to make you feel.

Kindah: I always like to think about how we interpret things with the set of tools that we've developed, and that's how we make sense of the world. And I just like to think about the unknown, how we don't know to label things yet. Maybe we are creating things that mean something, and we just don't know how to identify them.

Lisa: You have had people who've been critical of your work and say, "Oh, I could make that," or "That looks like a five-year-old made it!" This is a common response to super-abstract paintings.

Kindah: I just try and laugh at it. I have learned that's an uneducated response, because they haven't seen enough work to understand what goes into it. It's also very tempting to say, "No, your five-year-old could not make this," and then challenge them and have their five-year-old try and re-create it, and they of course won't be able to.

Lisa: What do you say to someone who says to you, "Okay, I want to become a professional artist, and I'm frustrated because I'm not making work that's very good yet."

Kindah: What is it, the ten-thousand-hours rule to become an expert? I made so many paintings that I didn't like and products that never sold. You have to go through that process and not look at them as failures, but instead look at all of it as taking steps to figure out what you really *want* to do. Very few times do things simply fall in your lap. You have to stay with it and ride through the ups and downs.

Lisa: When you are in a place where you are feeling tension or struggle, and you want to get to that place of joy or feeling again, what do you do?

Kindah: I realized at some point that I was going to have to make a lot of things that I didn't like in order to get to the stuff I did like. So now, I just try and push through discomfort. To get myself ready, I do warm-ups, just like with exercising. And a lot of my warm-ups are half-thought-out ideas, and I think that's a good way for people to kind of get in the groove. Sometimes I realize, "Ooh, I could've done this on a piece of paper first instead of going to the canvas." I think it's just like exercising. You have to work your way up.

THE ONGOING DESIRE TO CREATE

Once we experience the spark, most artists develop the desire to keep creating over and over again. It's almost a compulsion. That desire is essential, because without it, creativity can't manifest into anything tangible. According to researchers Kaufman and Gregoire, the spark—and the desire that arises from the spark—plays a role in helping artists persist through challenges and roadblocks that arise in the creative process and in life. As adults with free will, it helps to *want* to make something to actually make it, and we must have the will to stay with that desire itself, even when the process is challenging to our egos. What drives the motivation (and that is different for everyone) isn't as important as the desire itself. Making art as a regular practice is hard work, and beginning anything new can also feel vulnerable and even painful. So desire is essential.

It's possible that you occasionally lose the desire to create, or that you wax and wane through periods of desire and indifference. This is also a totally normal experience for creative people. It is also true that highly prolific creative people tend to force themselves to work through periods when they lack desire, or engage in exercises that awaken the desire when it feels dormant. If you're not feeling the desire for a prolonged period of time, it's important to consider whether the current expression of your creativity is really what you want to be doing or whether, instead, you should

Pink Pearl

change things up and be making something else or working in a different way. Listening to your internal desire (or lack of one) is critical to staying engaged with the creative process.

RISK-TAKING AND EXPERIMENTATION

We have all known people in our lives who talk constantly about what they are *going to make* someday when they have time or the right tools or skills, but who never actually make anything. Creative thinking happens in most people, but what differentiates most productive artists from the rest of the population is that they are compelled to *do* something with their ideas, and they are also usually able to work through fears about not being ready or not having the right set of tools. The urge is often so great that we improvise with the tools we do have, even if we don't have the perfect ones yet, and we make do with what skills we *do* have, even we aren't exactly sure how to make something.

At first, the urge to create takes the form of experimentation: trying out our ideas, even when we don't know how or where they'll go. Experimentation is where creativity comes to life. When you are experimenting, you aren't just thinking or talking about your ideas—you're actually *trying them out*. We don't just buy the supplies or watch the video tutorials and then stop. We actually create something. And we don't just do it once or twice. We do it over and over and over until we've developed some skill, or our desire to make that thing is satisfied, and we move on to experimenting with the next creative urge.

Sounds easy enough, right? If it were, we'd all be highly prolific. The truth is, when we first start something, it can feel wholly uncomfortable. It can even feel risky! What if we fail? When we have an idea for what we want to create (perhaps related to whatever gave us the spark and the urge to make something in the first place), the end result we envision is often so far from what we have the skills to do. So we get overwhelmed and feel almost immediately defeated. That's why many people, even when they first have the urge and begin to experiment, quickly abandon projects, because their taste level far outweighs their skill level. I'll talk about this more in Chapter 5.

Fortunately, most artists who have the stamina to work through the first few years of experimentation do become stealth experimenters. We not only become comfortable with the discipline of experimentation and the importance of failure, we also begin to crave it. It becomes part of how we work.

ANDY J. MILLER:
On Influences, Experiences, and Experiments

Andy J. Miller (aka Andy J. Pizza) is an American illustrator and public speaker. He is the founder of the *Creative Pep Talk* podcast, which gives pep talks to creative people. *Creative Pep Talk* has been featured by Apple, BuzzFeed, and Threadless. *Creative Pep Talk*, the book, was published by Chronicle Books in 2017. His explosive, color-drenched illustrations have brought hope and smiles to clients like Nickelodeon, Google, the *Boston Globe*, Converse, and Oreo. While studying in the UK, Miller received a BA in graphic design at the University of Huddersfield. He uses exclamation points liberally (!!!!), has been known to TYPE IN ALL CAPS for no reason at all, and sometimes uses emojis in business emails. The Pizza family lives in the great city of Columbus, Ohio.

Lisa: One of the greatest things about an artistic voice is that it's already in you. Every now and again, I'll try to do something that's completely different from what I typically do, and I can't get away from myself.

Andy: Yes! Your voice is part of your DNA recipe, which is in your blood and the code that makes you who you are. The combinations of little proteins in your blood are so infinite that scientists say there could never possibly be another combination like you. Even as humans evolve, the DNA sequences will change, and there will never be another one like you. Your voice is also your influences, your experiences, and your experiments. Those four things together make you this unique concoction and point of view and give you a unique narrative.

Lisa: It's hard these days to develop your voice when we are constantly influenced by other artists' work.

Andy: There's something out there by film director Jim Jarmusch saying that you should definitely copy, but only copy authentically. Only copy things that really, truly move you. Copying trends that don't move you or copying what you may think is critically acclaimed but that doesn't actually speak to you—that's the worst type of influence. Two years after graduation, I spent this season doing this self-exploration and trying to get rid of all my inauthentic influences. I tried instead to ask myself, "When I go look at art, what makes me feel something?"

Lisa: What do you think of the idea that it's better to emulate a movement rather than an individual artist, better to have many influences rather than just one or two?

Andy: I think a lot of creative people undervalue and underutilize the power of a movement. If you look back at the '60s and '70s, and you look at Seymour Chwast and Milton Glaser and Peter Max and all these guys, their work all resembled really clear core values that they were sharing and exploring together. They were part of a movement. And as an artist, you want to really dig into a movement. Don't be ashamed of learning from it and being part of that wave. Of course, at some point, if you're really going to take it to the next level and thrive, you're going to have to make some decisions that your heroes wouldn't make, and that is a really tricky time. There's a moment in *Star Wars* where Yoda tells Luke that his training isn't finished, and Luke says, "I don't care. I have to go save Han and Leia because they're in trouble." And he goes against his master's orders. At some point, your master and mentor can only take you so far.

One simple way to break away is to use different tools from what your heroes use. That was one of the things that helped me. When I got so entrenched in that doodle-based, line-work–heavy movement that I was in, I bought a Wacom tablet and started making shape-based stuff. So instantly, overnight, it looked a lot different, and I was forced to solve different problems.

Lisa: What about your experiences and experiments? How do those play into your artistic voice?

Andy: Those are all the things that happened to you in your life—they are yours and you own them. That's stuff that your parents did or stuff that you ran into along your life path. Whatever they are, you own those experiences. Your life experiences filter into your voice, even If you try to keep them out.

In the same way that you own your experiences, you own your experiments. The more you experiment, the more likely you are to have accidents that are fortuitous and lead to something new and positive. One of the formative things in the development of my voice was my "Nod" project, where I drew a new character every weekday for a year. I felt frustrated with my inability to move past my influences, and I thought if I just make a giant volume of stuff, I'm bound to accidentally force myself to just make stuff that ends up becoming habit and interesting and different and mine.

Lisa: You were obviously disciplined in your projects and that led to the development of your voice. Did you ever get bored?

Andy: There is a connection between boredom and creativity. As you're going along, you are trying to appease that boredom. And trying to get out of the boredom means that you have to invent new ways of approaching your work, and that forces you to experiment in different ways that you wouldn't otherwise. So many people I meet will be like, "I just want to be an illustrator so bad. I want to be a musician so bad."

And there is no way you can get to where you want to go without making piles of work.

Lisa: What about the importance of being uncomfortable and embracing the messiness of finding your voice?

Andy: When something feels uncomfortable, our subconscious tells us that we're doing something wrong. And that's funny because discomfort is more of a sign that you're headed the right way. When I look back on my own career, my work had to get a lot worse before it got better. I think some of the people who know my work now think, "Man, you have such a clear voice, and you have this really concise body of work and I want to do that." And I say, "If you go search my name and go look at my old work, there's a bunch of garbage out there. And I put that garbage out there to try to learn something."

Lisa: What advice do you have for anyone attempting to cultivate their voice who might feel frustrated that it's taking too long or that they need to fake it somehow till they find it?

Andy: Think of your artistic voice as the swag bag or reward that you get for attending the art party, but not as the ID that you need to get in. A lot of creative people think that they have to have their artistic voice sorted out before they start making art. In other words, before they go to the art party, they think that it's the ID that lets them in past the bouncers, so they can feel legitimate. And one of the things that happens is that because people think they have to have their artistic voice sorted before feel like they are a "real" artist, they either (1) give up and never start making art, or (2) they pretend to find their voice before they really have it. And that negates their ability to ever really find it, because you can't find something you already think you have. I think it was Epictetus who said something like, "You can't learn what you think you already know." So instead, we need to shift our thinking. You

don't need to have found your voice to attend the art party. Finding your voice takes years. Your voice is simply the reward, the swag you get eventually from attending the art party.

QUESTIONING

At least once, and probably many times on your path, you will encounter periods in which you question everything about your work. You'll begin to question the validity of your work, what it means, and even whether it's worth making at all. I went through a period of questioning several years ago that I liken to a dark existential crisis. Daily, for about two months, I was plagued by questions like, "Am I working on the right stuff? Is my work any good? Is my work meaningful to me anymore? What is this all for, anyhow?" I woke up nearly every day with feelings of ambivalence about my work, which, in turn, caused me to feel panic. As a prolific creative person who makes a living from her art, my work is everything to me, so if I questioned its quality or meaning, my whole identity as a human was in question!

Sound familiar? If so, you are not alone. I learned from sharing my experience with other artists that these periods of deadlock or insecurity are completely normal for artists. Not only are they normal, they can be really positive if we don't run away from them and if we confront the questions they force us to face. If we stay with our uncomfortable feelings they can be really helpful, and we can usually get to a place of flow again in our work.

My sense of angst and despondency about my work during this particular period made me realize there was probably some stuff under the surface that I needed to explore. So after a few weeks of unrelenting anxiety, I decided to dig deep into the impasse. I keep a journal, and there I forced myself to ask and answer a lot of questions, including "What am I afraid of? Did someone say something about my work that caused me to question it, or is this coming from my own sense of insecurity? What is the voice saying? Is it saying anything helpful? Or is it that insecure part of me that wants to keep me down? What are my hopes and dreams for my work? Why does my work feel stale? What can I do to feel good about my work again?" I also talked to trusted people in my life about how I was feeling, and asked for their perspective.

Sometimes periods of intense questioning are a signal that we need to temporarily walk away from whatever is irking us. So I also decided I needed to take a break from making art for a few weeks. It was near the holidays, and I found a spot in my schedule to take some time off. I am someone who draws and paints nearly every day, sometimes multiple times a day, even when I'm not "working" (I also draw when on vacation or at night while I'm watching TV), so taking a few weeks away from my art supplies and studio was a big mental shift. But I knew I needed some space to reckon with this period of questioning. In addition to sitting with my big questions, I forced myself to go outside into nature, to museums, and to places that inspired me. I brainstormed new ideas, made lists of things I was interested in, and delved into books and films in my areas of interest. Not only did I feel less angst when the break was over, I had a plan for moving out of the questioning phase. Not surprisingly, that period of questioning was followed by one of the most prolific and transformative years of my art practice. I fell back into a period of creative flow.

CREATIVE FLOW

Do you know that feeling when you are in the zone while you are making art? That's called being in your "creative flow." When you are in a period of creative flow, your concentration is laser-focused. Your self-consciousness disappears. When you are in creative flow, you lose track of time (five hours passes and it feels like five minutes). Your ability to create something out of the ideas in your mind happens with ease. The state of flow is described by some scientists as a deep brain-based impulse for creative stimulation, similar to our cravings for food.

Experiencing prolonged creative flow is an indicator that you're developing your creative voice. It can take years to get to a place where you experience regular periods of creative flow, and that's because when you are in learning mode, you're not yet fluent in your subject matter, style, or medium. It's like learning a new language, remember? Learning implies a certain amount of struggle, frustration, trial, and error.

But once you learn or master something, the struggle lessens and flow happens more frequently. Once you begin to experience periods of creative flow, you're likely not struggling as intensely with questions of *what to create* (subject matter, style) and *how to create it* (skill, control over your medium). To be clear, as an artist, you will *always* struggle. Bumping up against frustration, angst, monotony, and blocks are all part of the creative process. But once you have more experience, the challenging periods are not as difficult to move through as they can be in the beginning. The more "fluent" you become, the more you'll be in flow.

CHAPTER FOUR

NAVIGATING
INFLUENCE

Immature poets imitate; mature poets steal;
bad poets deface what they take, and good poets
make it into something better, or at least something
different. The good poet welds his theft into
a whole of feeling which is unique, utterly
different from that from which it was torn."

—T. S. Eliot

MIMICRY

You might occasionally ponder the big existential question, "Have I found my voice?" But on most days you are probably thinking about much more practical questions. Two of the most common questions we face in our day-to-day work are, "Is my work original?" and "How can I stand out as an artist?"

Navigating the influence of other artists in your journey to find your own creative voice is one of the most common points of tension—and that's because you can't actually find your own voice *without* being influenced by other artists. Save for a handful of outsider artists in the world who have little contact with other people or the Internet, it's virtually impossible. So the first shift is to think about influence as a positive thing, a *helpful* thing, and not something negative we need to avoid. Influence is actually critical to our development and growth. It's usually why we are inspired to make art in the first place. The key is what you *do* with that influence. Copying another artist's work explicitly and marketing or selling it as your own is not only morally wrong, it's against the law. Being influenced by artists and using that influence to develop your own voice, on the other hand, is a normal and healthy part of the creative journey.

INFLUENCE IS ALL AROUND US

Part of the reason it's impossible to develop your voice without influence is because art is everywhere. Art is on billboards and T-shirts, sneakers and magazine covers. It's all over the Internet, from social media to illustrations accompanying news articles and opinion pages. Everywhere we turn, especially with the easy, quick access we have to images of virtually every known artist, living or dead, we come into contact with and consume visual stimulation every single day, even when we don't intend to. We learn about artists and art movements in school and in books, we scroll through artists' feeds on Instagram, and we search for inspiration by artists on Pinterest. Our brain processes all of it as "I like that" or "that's ugly!" or "that speaks to me" or "nah, boring."

NAH, BORING.

We desire both to emulate those who inspire us *and* to be original. Bridging the gap between influence and originality is one of the most delicate lines we walk. In the introduction, I referred to this as the tension between standing out and fitting in, between nonconformity and conformity, and it can exist over the lifetime of our creative paths. As we discover the work of more artists, we cycle through new influences over and over again. It is essential to build an understanding of the boundaries that separate influence from imitation. Our goal should always be to get as far into our own corner as possible.

NOTHING IS ORIGINAL

In his book *Steal Like an Artist*, artist and writer Austin Kleon states emphatically that nothing is original. "What a good artist understands is that nothing comes from nowhere. All creative work builds on what came before." He's right. Nearly everything we create takes inspiration from something that has come before. Sure, we each have something new to bring, but we depend on the brilliance of minds that came before us.

This idea might stress some of you out. You might ask, "How in the world will I ever find my voice if nothing is original?" However, I hope reading this will actually make you relax. Understanding that nothing is original may help you to let go of the pressure to be completely original in the first place.

Fortunately there are some things we can do to consciously navigate influence so that we can get ourselves away from outright copying. First and foremost, let go of any idea you may have that you are immune from influence. No one is free from influence. Owning your influence is the first step!

STRATEGIES FOR NAVIGATING INFLUENCE

- Get to know and honor your influences. Bow down to them. Thank them. Write them letters of appreciation. Read about them. Ask them questions (even if they're dead), and imagine how they might answer. If you see art that you like for the first time, don't just grab the image and pin it on your inspiration board. Find out who created it. Research the artist's story; learn about where they find their inspiration and what drives their work. Find out who influenced them. The work that inspires you is part of someone else's creative journey. Begin to see the connections between the work you love and the artists behind it.

- Copy another artist if you need to see where that leads. Hey, that's totally fine. Go for it! Sometimes copying is a great way to push your skills or practice in a style that you admire. But when you make a piece of art that is directly and obviously inspired by another artist, always honor and give credit to the artist you copied. And never, ever, pass it off as your own for professional, paid purposes.

- Collect and use as many influences as you can. The more influences you have, the more of a fusion you'll create and the more diluted each of your individual influences becomes. When you have just one main influence you are far more likely to just be mimicking that one artist, whereas when you use many influences in your work, you are creating a mash-up, which means you'll ultimately be making something totally new. Only have one influence? Look for more! Is your influence part of a genre or movement? Explore that genre or movement for other influences that might inspire you. Collect many influences until you don't need them anymore.

• Make a list of your influences and what aspects of their work you admire. Each time you make art that draws from an influence, acknowledge it. Keep a growing list of all the artists you find yourself wanting to mimic. As you make that list, name all the things about each artist's work you idolize. Do you like their use of color? How they render figures? Their use of line work? The shapes they create? Then, be conscious of how you are transferring those influences into your own work. Always ask, "How am I transforming this influence into something of my own? How am I innovating?" And, if you are in the beginning of your path and you insist that you are making work that is *not* influenced by other artists, I urge you to go about digging deeper. Start by making a list of all the places you find your inspiration. Are any of those sources of inspiration movements in art or culture? Which artists are part of those movements? Remember, there is *no shame* in having influences! Matisse had them. Andy Warhol had them. I have them. You have them. Own them.

• Listen to your gut. Do you have that uncomfortable feeling that you are copying another artist's style and trying to pass it off as your own? Is it possible that someone else has pointed out that your work consistently looks like another artist's? Listen. Then go back and work on those pieces some more before you put them out into the world again. Add more of yourself or another influence. Change shapes and colors and lines. Push the work until it becomes something new.

• Spend periods of time off the Internet and out of books. If you are someone who relies heavily on reference or inspiration to begin a piece of art, try spending an entire week (or more!) making art that uses no reference or inspiration. Stay entirely off the Internet and completely out of books or magazines for gathering reference material. Notice what happens and how your work evolves.

• Research and find inspiration in really old art movements or eras in art. Instead of looking at contemporary art or your favorite artists on social media, look at medieval art and Renaissance art and folk art from the 1800s. Study works from ancient China or Egypt or Mexico or your own cultural heritage. Digging deep into centuries of art from all over the world will open up new directions, new ideas for pattern and color, symbolism and subject matter.

DANIELLE KRYSA:
On Consistency, Jealousy, and Persistence

Danielle Krysa has a BFA in visual arts and a postgraduate degree in graphic design. She is the writer-curator behind the contemporary art site *The Jealous Curator* and has curated art shows from Washington, DC, to Los Angeles and from San Francisco to Toronto. Danielle creates her own artwork as well, mixed-media collages that combine found images, paint, and as much humor as she can pack into each title. When she's not in the studio, Danielle is writing books; *Creative Block, Collage*, and *Your Inner Critic Is a Big Jerk* were the first three, and her fourth book, *A Big Important Art Book—Now with Women*, was released in October 2018. Danielle has also had the great pleasure of speaking at TEDx events, Pixar, Creative Mornings, and CreativeLive and has been interviewed for several video segments on *Oprah.com*.

Lisa: What does "finding your voice" mean to you as an artist?

Danielle: To me, "finding your creative voice" means creating a style or tone that people can recognize before they even see your name on the title card. Perhaps this is your color palette, drawing style, use of text, anything really. But the key is consistency.

Lisa: How do artists arrive at a distinct voice? What do they do to get there?

Danielle: Practice! Make a lot of junk, sort through the junk, pull out the pieces that feel like you—the work that makes you smile, makes you proud, and gets your creative juices flowing to make more. Toss everything else.

Lisa: How did you arrive at the artistic voice you have today? Where did you start and what led to the voice you have today as an artist?

Danielle: It's been a journey—a struggle, actually. I tried to get there a long time ago, but the Internet is so full of so much good work by so many other people that I found it really difficult to find my own voice. I wanted to be everyone else instead of myself. After all, their voices were already established, and as far as I could tell, they were perfect! I spent years trying to shake that off, to focus on my own work. The only way that happened was to make a lot of work. And then throw away a lot of work. Honestly, I found the way to myself by just focusing on being me in my studio.

Lisa: You had some experiences in art school that scarred you early on.

Danielle: Yes, I'd been told as a young art student that my work "should NOT be funny" if I ever wanted to be taken seriously as an artist. Needless to say, I cut out any and all humor from of my work. I was also told I "should never paint again" about five weeks before graduating as a painting major, so clearly I had no choice but to never use paint from that day forward. After decades of avoiding two of my favorite things—being hilarious and playing with bright, thick, luscious blobs of paint—I found my way back to me. It was a relief.

Lisa: Talk about finding your voice as primarily a collage artist versus a painter or someone who draws. What are the challenges associated with collage that might not exist for people rendering in other mediums?

Danielle: It is a bit tricky to find your own voice as a collage artist. A lot of us end up using similar-looking found images due to good old copyright laws (images need to be at least fifty to eighty years old depending on the country the images come from). Other than that, I think there are lots of ways to slice an image to make it your own, and you just really have to keep experimenting, pushing, and playing until you create work that is recognizably you. If you're not adding bits of your own drawings or paintings, it's hard to get "your hand" in there, but you can do that by the colors you choose to work with, unique compositions, scale, and so on.

Lisa: You've interviewed hundreds of fellow artists over the years on your popular blog *The Jealous Curator*. What stands out to you as the most important qualities in artists who have a very distinct voice and who are clear "nonconformers"? What is true about them as artists?

Danielle: They're not afraid to try new things. Failing isn't a word in their vocabulary—it's simply "experimentation." And when I've actually had the pleasure to meet some of these artists in person, you can almost instantly see how their personalities are present in their work. Granted, there are always a few who'll surprise you, but generally speaking their work is an extension of themselves.

Lisa: What role do you think social media plays now in helping or inhibiting artists early in their path?

Danielle: Social media can be overwhelming. After a few minutes on Instagram or Pinterest, you can walk away feeling like everything's been done in every color. But it hasn't. There is room for everyone, and you have to keep going. The positive side of social media? Using it as a tool. Monica Lee-Henell, an artist friend of mine, has some great advice on how to use Pinterest. She creates a bunch of boards themed around things she's drawn to, like landscapes, or portraits, or the color yellow. Then she pins like a crazy person in each of the categories! You might go into this thinking "a portrait is a portrait," but once you've created a full board, you'll start to see patterns emerge. Maybe you are most attracted to vintage portraits, or modern photographic portraits, or quiet graphite portraits. This smart trick helps you quickly turn your jealousy of everything else out there into a narrowed-down, much more focused recipe of the things you like. Now you have a starting place to make something uniquely you.

Lisa: What advice do you have for anyone attempting to develop their voice who might feel frustrated or defeated?

Danielle: I will never forget a particular experience I had where I had made an entire series of mixed-media pieces several years ago. My son was two, and he'd spend full days pretending to be a dog, or a dinosaur, or any other creature that popped into his amazing little mind. I was so inspired by him that I did a series of pieces featuring kids with animal heads. Clearly, I was a genius. About three months later, I started my blog, *The Jealous Curator*. While looking for content, within the first hour or so, I found at least five artists who were also putting animal heads on kids' bodies! *WHAT?* I hadn't copied, this was *my* idea, but still, it had been done before! I wanted to just give up, again. But I didn't. I realized that I just had to keep pushing past my first idea until I got to a new place that felt more unique, and that's what I advise people to do also. I don't regret creating that series, since it reminds me of those years at home with Charlie. And to be honest, a frustrating experience like that made me mad, but it also got me mad enough to get back into the studio to keep on working.

THE IMPORTANCE OF SHOWING UP,

PRAC-TICING,

AND SETTING ROUTINES

ON SHOWING UP

About seven years ago, I was asked to speak at a conference for creative entre-preneurs. The woman who ran the conference was an acquaintance I'd known socially in San Francisco, where I lived at the time. I used to run into her at nearly every event around town, from book signings to art shows to fundraisers for various causes. When she introduced me to the audience at the conference, she said the thing about me she admired the most was that I "showed up." It was the first time I noticed anyone describing me this way.

The compliment made me feel good, but it also caused me to want to explore this idea of showing up. I began thinking about it a lot. What did that mean exactly? And what were all the ways I was showing up? If it was a good thing to show up, how could I show up in new and different ways?

Maggie, the conference organizer, was complimenting me for *showing up* for other people. In so doing, I became part of a community of artists and creative entrepreneurs. I got to know folks who were also trying to make it in a creative field. I forged friendships with other people that led to the give and take of sup-port, idea sharing, and collaborations. Showing up for other people also meant that I immersed myself in the work of other artists, designers, and writers. I learned from them, which in turn helped me to gain perspective on my own work, important factors in developing my voice.

In my reflection, however, I realized that the notion of showing up was so much bigger than simply showing up for others in my community. Sure, showing up for and learning from other creative folks has a beneficial role in our development as artists. In my book *Art Inc.: The Essential Guide to Building Your Career as an Artist*, I talk about the importance of finding your community so that you can learn, share, and grow with other artists who are on a similar path. But I also knew that showing  up to work at my own drawing table was an equally valuable ingredient in the formula for artistic growth and success. If I spent most of my time looking at the work of other artists and hanging out at gallery openings, but not consistently making my own work, I might be inspired and make friends, but I'd never make progress in my own creative path.

Showing up includes putting in the work. Putting in the work can feel formidable, especially if you are just starting out and you have a job or a family and other commitments. Even when we have time scheduled in our day to make art, the fear of not knowing exactly where to begin or failing or experiencing boredom often keep us from starting. We make excuses for why it's not worth it to sit and work when we only have twenty minutes; so we choose, instead, to watch TV or scroll through social media on our phone. Showing up includes setting a schedule for making work, no matter how limited, and then doing the work consistently in that scheduled time. Your voice cannot develop in a vacuum. It is not the result of magical thinking or observation. Your voice develops as a result of showing up and making stuff, not once or twice, but over and over and over again.

PRACTICE ~~MAKES PERFECT~~ LEADS YOU TO YOUR VOICE

Once upon a time, I would wake up in the morning and walk bleary-eyed to my computer to check to see if I had gotten an email from my illustration agent about any new work assignments. I was just starting out in my career, and while I was lucky enough to sign with an agent just one year in, paid work came to me slowly at that time. There were weeks and weeks on end when I didn't have any gigs as an illustrator. Even though this was a bummer (and required living on a shoestring), I began to understand that if I was going to get to the place where clients were knocking at my door to work with me I had to make more work, and I had to make increasingly better and more interesting work. In other words, the only way I was going to develop my voice as an artist was through practice.

Showing up and making art every day is great, but practicing is next-level. Practice is about honing in on something specific—ideally the kind of work you'd like to get better at making—and then practicing that thing over and over. In some cases, that means (depending on your medium) practicing drawing, painting, photographing, or otherwise creating something in particular—like people, animals, specific forms, landscapes, or imaginary characters. In some cases, it's practicing the stuff you hope someone hires you to do in the future. One of the first tips my former agent, Lilla Rogers, gave to me was that I should give myself assignments when I didn't have paid work; I should use the time I had to make the kind of work I wanted to get hired to do by clients. That notion—*make the work you want to get as an illustrator*—became a mantra that guided my career. As a result, I experimented with practicing different types of illustration, including repeat pattern design, illustrations for the children's market, and drawing portraits of people. Instead of making just one or two of something, I made bodies of work, the accumulation of months of daily practice. Whether you have aspirations to be a professional artist or you want to make art for pure enjoyment, the habit of going deep with something through practice is a sure-fire strategy for speeding up the process of developing your artistic voice.

KATE BINGAMAN-BURT:
On Diving Deep, Finding Rhythm, and the Safety Net of School

Kate Bingaman-Burt is an illustrator and educator. Her work orbits around the objects in our lives: the things we buy, the things we discard, and the collectivity and social interaction that can arise from cycles of consumption. Via illustrations, daily documentation, publications, events, large-scale participatory projects, client work, and a full-time role as an educator, Kate's work invites a dialogue about contemporary forms of exchange. The building blocks of her practice include bright colors, hand-lettering, inventories of illustrated objects, and input and interaction from the communities of awesome people who contribute to her crowdsourced projects. Kate owns and operates Outlet, her studio, event space, zine library, and community Risograph print studio located in Portland, Oregon. Kate is an associate professor of graphic design at Portland State.

Lisa: What do people need to think about when they are ready to develop their voice?

Kate: People often look to other people to find their artistic voice, when they really need to ask themselves, "What is it that is unique about me? What different experiences am I made up of, and how can I make work about those things?" Ultimately, in the end, if you mimic another person's voice, it's going to fall flat. I think so much of it is realizing that your experiences are valid. Start by owning your story. I have this exercise that I do with my students that is about figuring out what is in your "creative family tree." The more branches your creative family tree has, the more unique your voice is going to be. Because if your creative family tree only has two branches, it's not going to be that unique.

Lisa: What are some examples of what would be on somebody's creative family tree?

Kate: One branch might be an interest in a certain style of illustration. Another branch might be this movie that has stayed with you for five years. Another branch might be all the cool things you collect from thrift stores. Another branch might be a particular interest in a period in history or weird experiences you had as a kid. And then you put that through your own filter and make a crazy, weird, custom smoothie blend through your art.

Lisa: In a way your voice is a melding of your various stories.

Kate: We love stories, and it's important to share your stories—what you love, what interests you, what repels you. If you dig deep enough, and you work hard at making piles of work, you're going to end up finding your stories. But to get there, you have to work on the story.

For example, I just had this conversation with a student; she's a brilliant illustrator, and she has so much to say. But for every single series she started, she would make just two pieces, and then she would talk herself out of that storyline and move on to something new. And I said, "You've got to be doing more than just two pieces around one idea. You can't talk yourself out of the whole project if you've only just explored it in two ways."

Lisa: Part of how you develop your voice is by exploring something in depth?

Kate: By diving deep, you're going to find a rhythm, you're going to discover patterns, you're going to discover new ideas, and I'm a firm believer that one project leads to another project leads to another project. Everything is connected, but you can't have that rhythm happening if you're only just kind of like, "I did two drawings." That isn't going to develop anything. You have to stick with a series and keep pushing it further, even if it feels awkward at first.

Lisa: What strategies do you recommend people use to commit to pushing a project beyond two or three pieces?

Kate: My personal experience is that, whenever I create a series or whenever I want to try something new, I am always thinking of a context or a home for where that series is going to live. So it's not like I'm just in my sketchbook trying something new. I think about context. For example, "I'm going to complete a new publication, and it's going to be about this idea, and I need to at least fill twenty pages for this publication," and so it's finding a home for your ideas.

Lisa: Basically, you assign yourself a deliverable. You're your own client.

Kate: Yeah. Maybe it's the graphic designer/illustrator in me, but I think about how my work is going to be applied and used, and who the audience is going to be. That way of thinking really helps motivate me to take a project from a sketch of an idea to something that is going to be a tangible object.

Lisa: Speaking of projects, let's talk about your well-known project, *Obsessive Consumption.*

Kate: My time in my MFA program was devoted to figuring out why people buy the things they buy and making work about that. It was originally about people and the stories behind their objects, and I documented it all through photography and interviews. I was taking photos in Target, thrift stores, Kmart, yard sales, and the like. One Saturday, I was documenting thrift stores, and I was taking photos and talking to people. I was also looking for a couch, and I photographed the one I was going to buy. And then it clicked: "Now I'm going to photo document everything that I purchase for the rest of grad school." That's where *Obsessive Consumption* began. Then, in October of 2004, I realized I had amassed a lot of debt, so I decided to confront my debt head-on, and that I would start drawing my credit card statements until they were paid off. And I picked drawing because I thought it would be a punishment. But I fooled myself because I really enjoyed the process! About two years into that project, I realized I wanted to make another project where I drew something other than my credit card statements, and then I began drawing everything I purchased. And then about a year into that is when I started getting contacted for illustration jobs, even though I'd previously had no ambition to become an illustrator. I had always thought of myself as a graphic designer.

Lisa: **You discovered that you enjoyed drawing, and then as you forced yourself through this project to continue to do it, you relaxed into it. And then you became known for that style, and now it's your career, in addition to teaching graphic design. It's fascinating to me how you didn't sit down one day and say, "I want to become an illustrator and hand-letterer."**

Kate: No. It was much more of an organic process!

Lisa: **How does your love for experimentation inform your point of view as you teach?**

Kate: In all the classes I teach, there is a lot of helping students develop their voices. I am always saying, "Please, whatever you do, I would rather see you do a huge pile of failure than do something that's not adventurous." If you use the analogy of finding your voice as a maze, I help students enter the maze, I give them a push if they need one to go in the maze, and I say, "Hey, don't worry, I'll be in here with you."

Lisa: You push them into the abyss.

Kate: Yes, and one of the beautiful things about being in school is that you can go into the abyss, and there's going to be someone, or many people, including classmates, there to help you through it. And when people ask me, "Do I need to go to school for graphic design?" I say, "You don't, but we do provide the safety net. In school, you have room to think of big ideas and fail, and someone's going to be there to help you, to help you sort through that mess, and that's not always the case if you do that entirely alone."

THE BEGINNER GAP

Practice can be fun for sure, but the problem is that very often our idea of the kind of work we want to make is way beyond our current skill level. There is literally a "skill gap" between our vision and our ability. One of my favorite descriptions of this gap is coined by *This American Life*'s Ira Glass. "All of us who do creative work, we get into it because we have good taste," he says. "But there is this gap. For the first couple years you make stuff, and it's just not that good. It's trying to be good, it has potential, but it's not." Glass goes on to say that realizing there is a gap between your taste (or your big ideas) and your skills is really disappointing to people, so they give up. "They quit," he says.

One of the challenges of being a beginner is continuing to show up and practice, even when your work feels like it doesn't match up to what you wish you were creating. Because the truth is, to get better at anything requires practice— doing the same thing over and over and over until we become a whiz at it. The good news is that with practice, your technical skills and your ability to work well in your medium will improve.

THE IMPORTANCE OF ROUTINE

There is a stereotype that haunts artists. It portrays us as disorganized, un-disciplined, and unable to keep a routine. And while a portion of the human population is disorganized, tardy, scattered folks (and many of them are artists), it is also true that not all artists are eccentric, chaotic, jumbled people. Many artists are super-organized and disciplined. And, on top of that, most people, even people who are innately disorganized, can learn to stick to a routine. In fact, regular routines are great for people who struggle with focus or organiza-tion. Putting boundaries around our time can help us to feel more in control of both our workload and the time we set aside for experimenting.

Setting a daily routine is important because the most direct route to cementing your technical skills and developing your voice as an artist is doing your thing—drawing, painting, sculpting, photographing, whatever—as often as you can for a designated period of time. Concentrated, regular practice leads to the fastest growth. In her essay "Harnessing the Power of Frequency," author and research-er Gretchen Rubin espouses working every single day, for long hours during the week, and for at least fifteen minutes a day on holidays and weekends. She posits that when you do something every day, starting feels less daunting, your ideas are always fresh, and it takes the pressure off, because doing a little bit every day is less stressful than cramming. She also says frequency assists the creative mind because staying engaged with your project on a regular basis keeps the spark lit. Lastly, she argues that frequency nurtures productivity. "Instead of feeling perpetually frustrated that you don't have any time for your project, you make yourself time every day."

MAKE A SCHEDULE AND STICK TO IT

To get into a routine of creating, I recommend making a weekly schedule that lays out when and for how long you will work on making art each day. For those of you who are already making art full time, scheduling can help you make sure you're allotting time for experimentation (and not just paid projects). If you have a job outside of your art practice or your schedule is otherwise limited, setting aside as few as fifteen minutes per day can help you to be more productive.

Then, at the beginning of each week, write down how you'll use each of the chunks of "art time" in your schedule. If you are freelancing and have paid, deadline-driven work, it's important to prioritize that first, but you also want to schedule time for personal work, learning, experimentation, and practicing new skills. You can even schedule time for developing your art business or taking classes.

Then make a habit of keeping to your routine like your life depended on it. Schedule all doctor's appointments, friend dates, and visits to the gym outside of the time reserved for art. Catch yourself when you feel like flaking on your routine. Thoughts like "I have no ideas today" or "I need to start over and I don't have the right canvas" are simply excuses to skip your scheduled time. It's imperative to take a no-excuses approach with your routine. Can't muster the energy to work on the drawing you started yesterday? Force yourself to sit down and free-doodle for the allotted time instead. Haven't figured out how to resolve the issues with the collage you worked on three days ago? Go back to another piece you need to finish and work on that instead. The idea is to show up and practice *something* during your scheduled art time. Chances are, once you begin, all your reasons not to sit down will fade away, and you'll get lost in the creative process.

SCHEDULE IN DOWNTIME, TOO

Getting lost in the creative process is great, and most of us wouldn't trade that feeling for the world. But the problem is that once we get into working, we might not stop. Make sure that your routine includes at least one or two solid fifteen- to ninety-minute breaks for taking walks, eating healthy snacks and meals, chilling out in front of a movie, spending time with friends and family, or hanging out with your art buddies. Those breaks will reenergize you for the periods in your routine that are slotted for disciplined work.

CHAPTER SIX

BEGIN ANYHOW: MOVING THROUGH FEAR

Everyone has talent. What is rare is the courage to follow the talent to the dark place where it leads.

—Erica Jong

FEAR AND THE CREATIVE PROCESS

Fear. While it can make us feel incredibly alone, nearly every human experiences it. It's also an integral part of the creative process. Making things and putting them into the world are requisite acts to finding your voice, and these acts often feel scary. And fears don't disappear as you venture further down your creative path. As we advance, we grow new hopes, dreams, and goals that create new standards for how we think our art should be received and the quality and volume of work we think we should be making. Those new goals and standards can lead us to new fears about what might happen if we don't meet them.

In this way, fear can sometimes motivate us to work hard. We think, "If I don't work at this, I won't get anywhere with it." So fear can actually be helpful on the path to finding our creative voices. But fear of failure or exposure or criticism can also paralyze us. For some people, fear takes the form of panic attacks or heart-racing anxiety. For others, fear is subtle and under the surface, always looming, easy to ignore temporarily if we simply distract ourselves from it. Or fear may pop up suddenly at unexpected times, just when things seem to be going smoothly. Of course, in all cases, fear *thinks* it's helping us: helping to prevent us from doing something that will embarrass or humiliate us or cause us stress or disappointment. But, in reality, what fear mostly does is trigger quitting, procrastination, and numbing behaviors that distract us from showing up fully to engage in the creative process.

SEEKING THE COMFORT OF THE "PERFECT MOMENT"

As creative people, we have *lots* of ideas. Our minds are swarming with them. But we also know that getting from our ideas to a final piece of art is a messy process. And that knowledge can make us feel overwhelmed, sometimes downright terrified. And so we sometimes wait for just the right moment to take action on our ideas: starting a new painting or a new daily project, a new illustration assignment, or a class to learn a more advanced skill. We fear if we start something before we're ready, we may look like an imposter, or someone else will be doing that thing better than we can, and we'll be reminded that we are not good enough. In the creative process, and really in life, we don't want to risk failing. We want to be *comfortable*. We want exactly the right skills, the right materials and supplies, the right knowledge, the perfect space in our busy schedule before we even *begin* something to minimize the chances that anything crappy will happen.

BEGIN ANYHOW

The problem is that, in the end, there is no perfect moment to begin. The creative process is usually messy, no matter how hard we try to make it clean and smooth. And sometimes "getting set up" becomes just an excuse not to begin. Don't get me wrong: I'm not knocking getting prepared. Having some good tools, some basic skills, a routine, and a quiet space to work are awesome and super helpful. But they *do not* prevent failures, challenges, and unexpected twists and turns. The stuff we take pains to avoid is just part of the experience of making art. The shift we need to make is to understand that those adverse experiences also help us learn and deepen our knowledge and strengthen our grit. "Risk and failure are essential components of meaningful creative achievement and, really, of any creative work," write Kaufman and Gregoire. Once we dive into the abyss a few times, we learn that what we feared is not actually that horrible after all. The challenge of the experience might even feel really good. So we have to take a deep breath, summon enormous amounts of courage, accept the messiness, and *begin anyhow*.

EMBRACE THE SUCK

Years ago, when I lived in San Francisco and I was just beginning my creative journey, I used to walk around the city and take pictures with my camera. It was a Nikon film camera, and I filled it with a special Fuji film that made super-saturated colors when the film was developed into prints. One day, I spotted a sticker that was slapped on a telephone pole. It said, simply, "Embrace the Suck." I photographed it, and instantly I knew: this was one of my new mantras. After I developed the roll, I stuck my super-saturated image of this red-and-white sticker on my inspiration board. I was, at the time, realizing that in order to become a fully developed person, I had to not just accept, but to embrace all the weird, annoying, inconvenient emotions that come with the creative process, including fear, self-doubt, vulnerability, and shame.

Moving through fear and other negative feelings and experiences requires accepting that they are a normal, natural, human part of the creative process. From the beginning of our path when we are uncovering our voice to the moment years later when we are firmly circling around in our own orbit, fear is trying to protect us from feeling bad. Self-doubt is trying desperately to keep us small and out of harm's way. But the problem is that if you succumb to fear or doubt (even with their lofty intentions), your creative journey will move either very slowly or, frankly, it won't move at all. To keep things moving, I like to speak directly to fear: "Thanks so much for doing your job! But I GOT THIS!" And then, instead of shoving fear out of the way (which isn't a bad strategy either), I imagine giving fear a big bear hug. My experience is that if we look our fears straight in the eye (instead of pretending they don't exist) and give them some love (or boss them around a little), they will lose their control over us. And, as a result, we will be more willing to enter the uncomfortable places and make more art.

LIBBY BLACK: On Mistakes, Engaging in Inquiry, and Magic

Libby Black is a painter and sculptural installation artist living in Berkeley, California. Her work is based on imagery culled from disparate sources like fashion magazines, snapshots, newspapers, and pop culture websites. She is interested in having the work chart a path through personal history and a broader cultural context to explore themes of imper-manence and queer identity. She has exhibited nationally, with such shows as

Bay Area Now 4 at Yerba Buena Center for the Arts in 2005; 2004 California Biennial at the Orange County Museum of Art, Newport Beach; and at numerous galleries in New York, Los Angeles, and San Francisco. Black has been an artist in residence at Headlands Center for the Arts in Sausalito and at Montalvo Arts Center in Saratoga. Her work has been reviewed in *Artforum*, *Art in America*, *ARTnews*, *Zink Magazine*, *Flash Art*, and the *New York Times*. She received a BFA from Cleveland Institute of Art in 1999 and an MFA at the California College of the Arts in 2001. Libby is an assistant professor at San Francisco State University.

Lisa: When you think about an artist's voice, what comes to mind?

Libby: Anybody can learn how to draw. It's what you do beyond the technical skill of drawing that makes you an artist. Your voice is what you can do with those skills and tools in your toolbox. Your voice is your ability to think critically, to question things. In order to make your voice grow, you have to keep feeding and taming it at the same time.

Lisa: The relationship we have with our artistic voice is complicated. The struggle to figure out who you are as an artist is hard, especially when you are first starting out. How should someone work through that?

Libby: By showing up and learning to be okay with mistakes. My students often say when they look at their work, "This is so bad." We're in a world right now where everybody is really fragile, and it's understandable. But I really try to foster this idea that making bad work is part of the process. And in my own journey through school and art school, my attitude was, *Just go to the studio and make the work and learn through making the work.* In other words, don't sit around and read theory and figure out what you're going to make based on Foucault or anything like that. I really believe that eighty percent of the work as an artist is showing up.

Lisa: You say developing your voice is like taming an animal.

Libby: I say to my students that we're going to learn some tools. We're going to learn contour and cross-contour and perspective and all these things. And then after that I tell them they can get more critical when they learn how to make something new with those skills. In the beginning it's like you're taming an animal. Except you're taming your voice.

Lisa: As artists, we're constantly working through our own perspective on whatever we're creating.

Libby: Yes. I come from a place where I try to make the work that I want to see in the world. In a way, that is inserting myself into the world and becoming part of the conversation. For example, I wake up, and I might get the Sunday *New York Times*, and read something in there that makes me want to remake the paper, like physically remake the paper or remix it with other images. And that's what I do. I am constantly responding to the world around me.

Lisa: How do you describe your work?

Libby: People think I'm just a sculptor, but I'm not even a sculptor. I'm a painter. There have always been paintings on the wall hanging out with my sculptures on the floor, but those sculptures are made from paper, paint, and glue. And that's what you make paintings out of, right? I began making sculptures of things because I wanted to be closer to what I was talking about. I really wanted the work to come as close as I could to the viewer and to be in relationship with them, and that was a way for me to do it. Previously, I was stuck in that rectangle or square.

Lisa: I think a lot of times artists get stuck in a medium or a particular way of doing something. We don't give ourselves permission to do something differently. We land in a box, very early on, even. "Oh, I'm a painter. I shouldn't delve into making three-dimensional objects." How did that shift happen for you?

Libby: Yeah, I remember exactly. I was in graduate school and Jim Hodges was a visiting artist at CCA, and he questioned me, "Why are you painting this on a wood panel? Why is it just on the wall? Why isn't it on the floor? Why is it made out of this material?" I mean, it's the why, why, why that is the critical thing, still. He kept asking me, you have this idea, and what is the best material to convey it? For me, that opened up so much.

Two weeks before my MFA show, I turned down a different road. I emailed my dad and I said, "Can you take pictures of mom's shoeboxes?" My mom had fifty-one shoeboxes in her closet. This was seventeen years ago, and he was new to the Inter-

net, and he took four boxes at a time. He emailed photos of them to me, and they were blurry as hell. But I re-created life-size versions of all those fifty-one shoeboxes, and that was my MFA show. And I remember thinking, "Libby, you are two weeks away from this show," and I was completely mortified and fearful. But from that moment forward, every time I'm feeling that way, I know something great is going to happen, or there's going to be a lesson that I am about to learn. If you can crack some of the doors to have that freedom, that's where the magic is in making art.

Lisa: How do you ensure that your own work continues to evolve after you've been making art for so long in your practice?

Libby: I do painting, sculpture, and drawing because I get bored if I do just one thing.

Lisa: It's amazing how many artists can focus on one thing.

Libby: Yes, and the threat of that—that I will only do one thing forever—is part of what motivates me to work in so many ways. What was great about getting to know Jim Hodges when he was at CCA was that he would make something out of porcelain, and the next day draw a flower on a napkin, and the next week make a big quilt.

One summer I started to make this larger sculpture, and I realized after I started that I didn't want to waste the whole summer on one sculpture.

So I got a bunch of eight-by-ten wood panels and I made eight paintings, and it filled my studio up in this way, and then I could focus on these bigger pieces that take a longer time. I grow my voice by doing both things that are long-term and tedious and also things that are faster and easier and more immediately satisfying. That combination keeps me in conversation with my work; there are parallel lines running all the time: pencil drawings, gouache paintings, sculptures, and then the bigger acrylic paintings. That, to me, is like a thick-layered sandwich; they all need each other, and I'm having a richer conversation with the work, and it keeps my interest and the time line of my work exciting.

Lisa: Do you grapple with self-doubt?

Libby: Absolutely. It's part of the process. There is magic when you make a painting or a sculpture at times. Sometimes I'm just like, "I made this paper chair out of paper!" Now, in the beginning of the process, before I finish something, I'm usually saying to myself, "This sucks, Libby, this sucks, this sucks, this sucks," but then I keep going. And then two hours into it and I'm like, "It's OK. You're making it. Oh my God, it's standing up. Oh my God, it looks like a chair. Oh my God, you painted that!"

Sometimes we start like we've never actually made a piece of art before. It's the weirdest thing. We beat ourselves up before we even start. We crush ourselves. But if we keep at it there is something that appears. There are moments where I don't want to be in the studio, and I have to tell myself, "Get off your ass, Libby, and just go in there and put a coat of paint on something because that will make you stay a little bit longer."

Lisa: If you can force yourself to do something for fifteen minutes, chances are you'll continue to do it for forty-five minutes to an hour, at least. It's the first fifteen minutes that are the hardest. Beginning is the hardest thing.

Libby: Do you know who Sally Mann is? Did you ever see *What Remains*, the documentary about her?

Lisa: Yes!

Libby: I watch that all the time, when she's in the car and she just got done with that big show and she's like, "What do you do? You just pick up the camera and take the next picture. And I'm usually the one standing there, so it's like a self-portrait." It gets me every time, because that's it. You're trying to up yourself from the last piece, but you're also just trying to get in there in one piece and leave in one piece.

FEAR IS ALSO WHERE THE MAGIC HAPPENS

For me, one of the most poignant moments in Libby Black's interview is when she told me about her experience in graduate school, as she abandoned her plans for her final exhibition at the last minute for a brand-new, more compelling idea. She was terrified, but she went with it anyhow, and it changed the course of her work forever. She says now whenever she feels fear in the context of her art practice, she knows she's onto something good. "If you can crack some of the doors to have that freedom, that's where the magic is in making art." Fear is often an indicator that we are onto something brilliant or new, some unexplored territory, something that will rock our world or the worlds of other people. If we reframe fear as an indicator of risk—and an essential element in the process of finding your voice—it is possible we can begin to see it as a positive sign, and even get excited about it.

Once we're in the messy, hard, or dark place we were trying to avoid, we realize that the messy, dark, hard part can also be the most interesting, and if we sit for a prolonged period in the discomfort of it, it's often where our best work comes from. It's always where we learn. Ultimately, it's where the magic happens.

WHEN BAD THINGS DO HAPPEN

But what about when our fears come true? What about when we make something we hate or that doesn't meet our expectations? What happens when we make something we like but a client or some other person whose opinion we value tears it apart? Our first reaction might be to want to walk away or quit. Feelings of shame are, at best, really uncomfortable, and most of the time they are incredibly painful. They give us anxiety. ("Ugh, maybe I am not meant to be an artist!") They make us feel defeated. ("I'll never get there!") They cause us to compare our paths and our work to others. ("I'll never be as good as so-and-so.") They make us feel embarrassed. ("I want to crawl in a hole and never come out.") In addition to wanting to quit, we also want to escape our feelings—by eating or drinking, by shopping or scrolling through social media.

The good news is that those uncomfortable feelings are not going to kill you. If you begin to expect them and manage them as a necessary part of the creative process, feelings of anxiety and defeat can actually serve a purpose in helping you to find your voice. They can be an indicator that you need to work on something to improve your skills. Conversely, they can be an indicator that your work is actually moving or changing, which is always a signal that you are doing something innovative or different. This idea goes back to the tension we experience between conforming versus being someone who stands out of the crowd. In theory, we want our art to stand out. But we are also terrified of that, because we risk pushback or criticism. Most career artists, out of necessity, become, over time, accomplished at feeling uncomfortable. "To generate and share original ideas in a world that is distrustful of creativity requires a certain bravado," write Kaufman and Gregoire. "To not only generate but to share nontraditional ideas, one must be willing to be a bit of a troublemaker and risk being labeled an outsider." Garnering the courage to continually push your work further and further into its own corner and out of the safe zone will only strengthen your artistic voice over time.

CHAPTER SEVEN

STRATEGIES FOR DEVELOPING YOUR OWN VOICE

LET'S GET PRACTICAL

By now you've probably gotten to the point in the book where you're thinking: "I get it! To find my voice, I need to show up, make art every day, practice the stuff I want to get good at, and give my fears a big bear hug." If you've got that much so far, you're already on your way. But there are some really practical things you can do and shifts you can make in your thinking that will nurture—and possibly even speed up—that process. In this chapter, you'll find loads of practical hands-on practices and adoptable mindsets that will lead you to your voice.

MAKE ART EVERY DAY, EVEN FOR A FEW MINUTES

The most direct route to developing your voice is getting into a routine where you make art every single day. The results will be faster if you engage in periods of focused practice in a particular medium or subject matter. Andy Miller talked in his interview about his "Nod" project early in his career, during which he drew a new character every weekday for an entire year. He knew that if he made a giant volume of new drawings, he was bound to break away from his influences and make stuff that ended up becoming "habit and interesting and different and mine." Not only did that project help Andy find his own voice, it also helped to propel his professional illustration career forward by filling his portfolio with the best from the project.

WHEN IT GETS HARD, DON'T STOP—*KEEP GOING*

Here's the thing. As much as it can be enjoyable and relaxing, making art, especially when we engage in it a lot (and aspire to get better at it), can feel ridden with anxiety, tedium, or frustration. This is especially true when we are beginners, when we don't always have the skills or tools to execute our ideas. It can leave us feeling disheartened and defeated, thinking things like, "I can't do this" or "Maybe I'm not cut out to do this," which, in turn, makes us feel like quitting. But when that happens, it's all about hanging in there. In my book *Art Inc.*, I talk about a former painting teacher of mine who used the analogy of the "painting curve." At the beginning of the painting curve, when we first start a painting, everything looks great. But as we lay down more paint, things can become muddy, and we inevitably paint over the previously good-looking parts of our painting. This is the bottom of the painting curve. If you can continue to work the painting (or whatever your medium), adding more layers, working through creating depth and dimension, finishing with the details, most of the time you'll head back up the other side of the curve. The process of creating almost anything (and not just paintings) has a messy period where things feel like they are falling apart and we want to rip up the piece and throw it in the trash. But if you can work through that period, you are more likely to make a more refined, more complex piece of art in the end. Working through the bottom of the curve is essential to finding your voice. So get comfortable with feeling frustrated and keep going. It's part of being an artist.

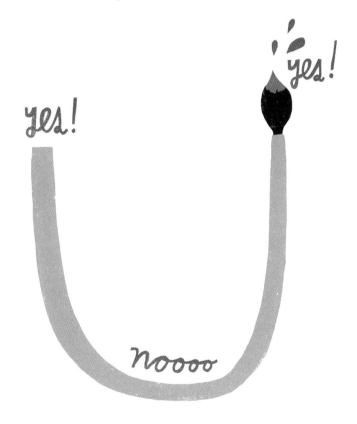

EMBRACE THE MONOTONY

Making art can stir up a whole host of uncomfortable feelings, and tedium and boredom are no exception. And that's because finding your voice requires showing up to practice, but practice often involves doing the same thing over and over and over. Finding ways to honor, appreciate, and enjoy the tedious aspects of your work will help you enormously in your path. For example, my friend, cartoonist Nicole Georges, dreads drawing trees, because by the time she's drawn the two-hundredth leaf, her brain is so fatigued and her hand aches. But she can't avoid drawing them, because they are an essential element in her work, since many of the scenes in her graphic novels take place outside. Over time, Nicole has learned to relax into the process of drawing trees, and even when she feels irritated, she doesn't give up. She told me that's because she knows all that tedious work leads to a beautiful tree, and in the end she feels a sense of pride and delight in her trees. Just like the dark places can sometimes lead to magic, so can the monotony. The key idea is to find ways to relax into the stuff that feels slow or not immediately satisfying. This can be as simple as listening to your favorite music or podcast, drinking a warm cup of tea, finding a cozy spot to work for the day, or, like Nicole, getting excited about where all the tedium is headed.

Monotony can also have the added benefit of forcing us to change our process or add new elements to our work. Sometimes we become so excruciatingly bored with a daily challenge or some seemingly endless aspect of our process that we end up changing our course (and work) in some way, simply to make the act of creating less painful. Ayumi Horie uses boredom to trick herself into innovation. "Pottery is intrinsically repetitious," she told me. So she sets up what she calls "a numbers game," where at some point she makes so many of the same thing and becomes so bored that she is "forced to try something new." In a way, boredom is essential to innovation. Boredom forces us to think of new or experimental ways to speed up or change our process (or the work itself), or, like Libby Black, to create new work in tandem with the monotonous work so that, as a whole, our work feels more exciting to make.

AYUMI HORIE:
On Boredom and Using Your Voice for Justice and Change

Ayumi Horie is a full-time studio potter in Portland, Maine, who makes functional pottery with drawings of animals and typography, inspired by American and Japanese folk traditions and comics. In 2015, she was awarded a Distinguished Fellow grant from United States Artists and was the first recipient of *Ceramics Monthly*'s Ceramic Artist of the Year award in 2011. She cofounded The Democratic Cup, a political project promoting civil conversation, and runs Pots in Action, a curatorial project on Instagram that features global ceramics. She co-created Portland Brick, a collaborative public art project that repairs city sidewalks with bricks stamped with past, contemporary, and future memories of Portland, Maine. She has organized multiple online fundraisers including Obamaware in 2008 and Handmade for Japan in 2011, which has raised over $100,000 for disaster relief. Recently, Ayumi was included in two books: *In the Company of Women* and *Handcrafted Maine*. She is currently a trustee at the American Craft Council and Haystack Mountain School of Crafts.

Lisa: Where does an artist's voice come from?

Ayumi: I think that there's this myth that creative voice is divine inspiration. A lot of my work is trying to debunk the myth of the creative genius. Your voice isn't something that appears out of nowhere or that appears when you finish art school. Your voice is this mix of stuff that's happened to you, how you process things, what you love, what you aspire to be. All of those things take a really long time and require hard work to develop. Artists have agency about what they want to explore, let out, and cultivate. You can also add privilege into that mix. Some of us were lucky enough to be born with some privilege, whether it's economic or family support. Privilege includes those things that have allowed us to explore and pursue our creative voice. Many people don't have that privilege.

Lisa: Why is it important to develop your voice as an artist?

Ayumi: There is a correlation between having a distinctive voice and voicing your truth. Voicing your truth is important because it gives us power as individuals—in particular, as women, as people of color, as queer people, those with different abilities. In a broader sense, it gives power to anyone who believes in justice. It means exploring our own humanity. Equally valid and essential is working within cultural and historic traditions, especially indigenous and nondominant cultures. It's a form of both cultural preservation and resistance, and we need these voices more than ever today.

Lisa: Let's talk about your story. When did you realize you wanted to be an artist, and what has your path been since?

Ayumi: I would put myself in the camp of the kid who loved art but never saw it as a legitimate way to exist in the world. I did major in studio art in college. I got out of school, and I worked as a professional photographer for a couple of years until I decided I wanted to be a potter. I was twenty-five by the time I went back to school.

Lisa: You went back to school specifically to study ceramics?

Ayumi: It took many years, but eventually I went back and got an MFA in ceramics at the University of Washington. At the time, it was known as a figurative school and a place that didn't really care about function. I said, "This feels like a place that will really rock my boat," which it did. The process of having to defend my ideas made me much clearer about who I was and what I cared about. Of course, having to defend my ideas was also painful, but ultimately, it caused me to be able to separate my work from who I am as an inner being. And that caused my work to continue to grow and change.

Lisa: How did the rigor of the MFA program impact the direction of your work?

Ayumi: It allowed me to give shape to something that had always been there. It's not this thing that's just like a magical *poof!*, and all of a sudden you go to art school and have your voice. It's a process of raking through your life to figure out what's important to you. It was probably the first time I'd really thought about the duality present in my life. Like the fact that I grew up in a Japanese household in the middle of a very white state, and what it meant to my identity to reconcile an American side of me and a Japanese side of me. It took grad school to wrestle with all of the rich content that is still feeding my work. That's something that's fairly obvious, but there are other things that are less obvious.

Lisa: What are some of the less obvious things you wrestled with?

Ayumi: Drawing from my experience as a kid. Refusing to wear dresses. Putting my foot down as a kid and saying, "I don't want this aesthetic. I want to wear sneakers and wear a big belt buckle, and I don't want to play with dolls." I draw from my experience as a child standing up for myself, and that resurfaces over the years into what I do now. Parts of being a kid felt really crappy. So I ask, what can I do now to speak to that experience or give other people the strength to make their own choices about their lives? That is part of my voice.

Lisa: What happened when you emerged from the MFA program?

Ayumi: It was right when the Internet was taking off, and so I thought, "Oh, this seems like a really viable approach to both being able to make a living and to be creative." There weren't any templates back then for a website, so I learned how to code so I could figure out how I wanted to express my ceramic work online. I liked the idea of being able to make the quirkiest thing I could and still have an audience for it, because it takes just one person to like that weird raccoon cup. All my photo experience came back into play. For a long time I had dropped photography, but then it became an important skill to have with the Internet. In addition to making and selling my work, within a few years I launched Pots in Action, which, at first, was this project about crowdsourcing images of my pots being used, so that it might close this loop between maker and user. But then, it has more recently evolved into an Instagram feed, which is about global ceramics generally. We tackle different themes. So it allows me to be an artist who works alone in Maine and also to be deeply connected with the world and to respond to what's going on in it.

Lisa: What is your work about?

Ayumi: Well, at its most basic level, it's about opening up the softer side of a person. I use cuteness as a strategy. In a lot of ways, I'm making these security blankets that I hope will give people a little bit of courage to do what they need to do in the world. I feel like everybody needs a place to come back to where they feel safe and good, and I'm hoping I am offering that, both through the way the objects feel—the weight of them, the way your hand fits inside a handle—and the surface texture or the imagery on them.

Lisa: How do you continue to develop your voice as an artist?

Ayumi: One thing I do is that I set up a system of boredom. Pottery is intrinsically repetitious. On one hand, staying engaged with the variations or the idiosyncrasies of a certain piece can be interesting, but sometimes, it's just boring. So I like to set up a numbers game, where at some point, it just feels like, "Oh my God, I cannot do this thing in the same way again!" And so I am forced to try something new. I also constantly work on trying to acquire new skills. For example, tomorrow I'm going to take a Premiere Pro class. I'm trying to continue to improve my foundational skills, so that I can be a better craftsman. For me, the quality of how something is presented is as important as the subject itself. I also pay attention to the things that I love and I think about how to integrate them into my work. I think, "Oh, how can I do that in my way?" Or, "Boy,

I've been thinking about that thing for twenty years. Maybe it's time to finally explore that thing."

Lisa: You mentioned earlier that an important aspect of being an artist is responding to the world. I know you are influenced by what's happening in the world, and using that as motivation to make meaningful work.

Ayumi: In some ways, that's the most important way to keep evolving as an artist. For example, there is so much outrageous stuff happening in the United States right now that if I let in enough of that stuff, it causes me to want to work toward justice. I think that we need to take care of ourselves because it can absolutely be overwhelming and exhausting, but I also feel like it can be this wonderful motivator for trying to put something positive out into the world.

Lisa: What advice would you give to somebody who's in that position in the beginning of their path and struggling to find their own voice?

Ayumi: Part of finding your own voice is being active and deliberate about it. But I also think the bulk of it is arrived at indirectly. I think it comes from carving out time and space and protecting that time and space from distraction. It means putting your phone in another room and not scheduling other things during that time. I get my best work done when I have a big block of time without distraction, or when I'm at a residency. These days, it takes so much work to block out the world. Inevitably, something will come out of that investment. It might take years, but it's something that can't be hurried. There is no magic pill. It's about discipline.

Lisa: You and I both come from backgrounds where we identified as "jocks" when we were younger. We've both used the sports analogy to describe our penchant for discipline. Talk about that.

Ayumi: I'll admit, I'm not really into sports as much now, but as a kid, learning how to practice a skill, even if it was something like foursquare in the schoolyard, was so important, something you just did every recess.

I feel like that sense of practicing to get better at something gets built into your system, and that has served me well.

Lisa: I think music is another good example. If you want to become a good pianist or a good guitar player or a good violinist, we understand that practice goes into that. Art is no different.

Ayumi: Yes, and there's an inherent value in loving to do whatever your thing is—whether it is art or music or sports or all of them—to the point that you have the desire to put in the hours to become better at that thing. You may not be the most famous artist that ever lived, but there is this value of deriving joy from whatever it is that you do. That's just good enough. We can't ask for much more than that.

CREATE CHALLENGES FOR YOURSELF AND STICK TO THEM, NO MATTER WHO IS PAYING ATTENTION

I like to think of personal challenges as the backbone of the development of your artistic voice, and that's because when you focus in for a period of time on making a body of work, practicing a particular technique, or using a particular medium, your skills and style develop. Sometimes personal challenges take the form of creating a cohesive body of work—a set of paintings, sculptures, collages, photographs, ceramic pieces, repeat patterns, drawings (or a combination of many things)—that you make around a similar theme for a period of time. Sometimes personal challenges take the form of a daily or weekly project where you create something specific every day for a set period of weeks or months. For example, in order to get better at drawing portraits, you might draw a portrait a day for a period of weeks or months. You might use a particular set of constraints, like using a new medium or the challenge of drawing something in under ten minutes. Employing constraints is a great way to build dexterity and boost innovation, because working with limits forces you to problem-solve and think outside your usual way of doing things, much like monotony does. In 2016, I worked mostly in the color blue for the entire year. Not only did I create over seventy-five paintings, drawings, and collages held together by color, but working in monochrome also forced me to think outside my normal bag of tricks about how to make my subject matter work as I played with a limited palette of shades and values.

Undertaking personal challenges also takes the preciousness out of your work. They push us out of the mindset that says every piece of work we make needs to be a perfect, finished piece. When you consistently create a large volume of work over time, it becomes obvious very quickly that each of your works is actually an experiment, and not every one of them needs to be successful or ready to hang in a show. Yet, over time, as you look back over your project, I guarantee you will see your work (and your voice) sharpening and developing. And, inevitably, when you work in this way, you'll period-ically produce a few pieces that are really successful (and potentially even path-changing)—another marvelous payoff.

MARTHA RICH: On Staying Weird, Setting Challenges, and the Power of Tangents

Martha Rich graduated with honors from Art Center College of Design in Pasadena. Her commercial clients include Blue Q, Honeygrow, Wieden+Kennedy, Penguin UK, Chronicle Books, Sally Morrow Creative, the *Pennsylvania Gazette*, *Rolling Stone*, *Entertainment Weekly*, *McSweeney's*, *Portland Mercury*, Y&R, the *Village Voice*, *Bon Appétit*, *San Francisco Chronicle*, Henry Holt & Co., and Country Music TV, to name just a few. Her work has been featured in the Beck video "Girl," and the book *Sketchbook Expressionism* features artwork from her sketchbooks, published by Murphy Design. Rich's artwork has been shown in galleries throughout the United States and internationally. She is currently living in her hometown of Philadelphia, after receiving her MFA in painting from the University of Pennsylvania. Rich teaches classes at the Fashion Institute of Technology and Tyler School of Art.

Lisa: What's a creative voice?

Martha: You can't control your creative voice. It just comes out of you. Most of the time I'm not "aware" of the voice that's coming out of me until after it's already out. It's the things you're naturally drawn to. Colors. Topics.

Lisa: As much as you try to avoid your voice, you can't.

Martha: Exactly. I remember being in school and struggling, trying to do all this stuff that you're assigned to do and trying to make my work a certain way, and then these little weird things would just come out. "I'd rather draw a bra, and I'm going to try to figure out how to put that into this other context." It comes out naturally. It forces its way out.

Lisa: Why do you think having a distinct voice is important?

Martha: I think it's definitely what sets you apart from everybody else. If you want to have a career where people are seeking you out as you, it's critical. It separates you from the rest of the crowd . . . if you want to be that kind of artist where people say, "Oh, Martha Rich, she does weird speech bubbles, and that's what I want for this specific project." I think that's kind of the cool thing about it. You're the same, Lisa. Your work is personality-driven—people are seeking out "a Lisa," you know? It's about what you can add to the conversation. Your audience, your clients, they want something that's coming from you, and that only you can do. It's cool.

Lisa: What was the spark that led you to be an artist?

Martha: I've always been artistic from the very, very beginning. I just didn't realize that it was something you could do for a job in life. We had this room in our basement growing up that was just for crafts. It was the seventies and there was macramé down there. My mom had photography equipment, and she taught my brother and me how to develop film. We had an enlarger, and she would make prints, and we would tumble rocks and make stained glass and do batik. I've been making art ever since. It was just part of life. I just figured that's just what you do. But then, I lived in the suburbs, and you go to college and get a liberal arts degree and a job. Nobody said, "Hey, you can be an artist when you grow up!"

Lisa: So what changed?

Martha: I ended up moving around in corporate jobs, I got married, and I moved to California with my husband. We were there for about a year, and then we ended up going through a divorce. And I didn't know anybody, I was kind of miserable, and I said, "I'm going to go take some art classes to keep my sanity."

Lisa: How old were you at this point?

Martha: I was thirty-five. So I was working at Universal Studios Hollywood in the human resources department in a little teeny-tiny cubicle, and I listened to the WaterWorld show like three times a day because my office looked over the back lot. And I said, "Oh my God, what am I doing?" I saw my whole future. Everything that I thought I was supposed to do didn't happen. So I began taking classes at UCLA extension. I realized then that I had a knack for art. Somebody told me about Art Center College of Design. And they have a night program, so I took classes there. I wanted to be a graphic designer. So I took a graphic design class, and then I saw another class for illustration, and it was taught by the Clayton brothers. So I took that, too. And when I started the classes, I knew like instantly that I was not going to be a graphic designer because you have to measure things, and there's kerning, and it wasn't me. I'm sloppy. So the illustration class just hit me. I couldn't wait to go to that class every week. And they were really, really supportive and encouraging of me and kind of basically said, "You should quit your job and go back to school." I had nothing to lose, so I said, "Okay." I applied to go to Art Center using drawings that I made while I was sitting in jury duty, and they accepted me. I don't know how I did it. I don't know how I paid for it. And from there to where I am now, twenty years later? It's crazy. I can't believe I've been doing this for—well, eighteen years since I graduated.

Lisa: How did you come to make the kind of work you're known for now?

Martha: It didn't take me very long to go from doing traditional editorial illustration, which is what I learned at Art Center, toward the way I work now, drawing and painting shapes and things. I like eavesdropping, and I started bringing that into my work. It's a very weird natural process that I don't notice as it's going on, but then all of a sudden, I said, "Oh, I'm making wood cut-out speech bubbles." It's weird. It's awesome.

Lisa: So you listen to what people are saying, and then do you actually write those things down? Do you have a notebook?

Martha: I do. I have a little notebook that I write in, and if I don't have my notebook with me, I have pages on my phone in the memo section of stuff I hear because otherwise I'll forget. People want me to make speech bubbles. I'm doing lots of murals with speech bubbles.

Lisa: Are you a planner, or do you work in the moment?

Martha: If it's a paid job for a client, I definitely have to plan, but it's not my natural state of being. Sometimes, it's very hard. I am naturally a spontaneous person. Most of the time, I get supplies out and I start making something. Sometimes what I do comes out of my need to be practical. For example, I paint a painting, and there's paint leftover. It drives me nuts. I hate wasting paint, like if I put it out on a little palette. So I had the *New York Times Magazine*—I was getting the Sunday *Times* for a while, and so I'd save the magazines. And I started using the leftover paint. I just would make shapes over the type in the magazine, and that led to a whole bunch of new work. Random experiments like this are always leading to new work for me.

Lisa: Let's talk about all the things you do, from illustration to murals to fine art. What does it do for your practice to have such a diverse repertoire of clients and projects and ways that your work goes into the world?

Martha: It keeps me from being bored. I love that I'm not set in one certain way of working. There are some people who gain success early on for a very specific look, and then they're potentially stuck in that and it's harder for them to break out. I think I come across as being an experimenter, and it makes it so I've always got some sort of interesting new thing to do. I went from doing editorial illustration to doing some book covers to doing an album cover or doing a thing in a video. Having that large grouping of different things makes people not afraid to ask me to do something that might be a little bit different than what they've already seen. I think that maybe is just from doing this so long. People trust you because they can see that you produce work that's interesting. I love that it's growing and going in different directions. I don't even know how to define myself. I don't really know what I am. I'm just making stuff. And I'm open to trying new things. I've carved out a nice little career doing different things.

Lisa: How do you ensure your own artistic voice continues to grow?

Martha: I always like to make up challenges for myself. The big one that changed a lot of stuff was when I did a painting a day for a year back in 2006. That forced me to come up with an idea a day within a certain amount of time. I give myself challenges, and that stuff is what changes you. If you're always just relying on what you already know, that's when you get stale. So I also like to say yes to things, like if somebody comes to me and says, "Can you just do a show in my space?" Or "Do a painting for me to help fundraise for my school." I always say yes. I'm not worried about selling it that much. So I'll just make some kind of weird thing, see what happens.

Lisa: It seems like your openness to new experiences has really contributed to the development of your voice. You are also known for your weird subject matter. Where do you get your ideas?

Martha: They come from traveling a lot and going to visit people and exploring areas. I become obsessed with a topic, and then I'll do research on it, and then work comes out of that. When I was in school, one of the things I became obsessed with were the people who handle snakes in church, like in the Appalachian mountains. So I did a whole series of stuff on the Appalachians. It comes from little things from my past, from what I see on the streets, from where I go to visit. I'll find some weird little thing that I think is cool, and then from there, something else comes out of it.

Lisa: What advice would you give to someone in the beginning of an artistic path who's having angst like, "I don't think I have a voice. Will I ever be able to develop one?"

Martha: You have to stop thinking about it, which is the hardest thing for an artist starting out. You have to trust in the process. Just keep making stuff and let go of caring if it looks crappy. Don't be afraid to fail. The minute you think about trying to have a style, STOP! It's really hard. I don't know how to tell somebody to do that because I was like, "It'll come to you." It's sort of like saying, "May the force be with you." You won't know it until it happens, but you have to just keep making work and keep trying. The work is the most important thing, and the stopping of thinking about it too much. Make work, go off on tangents, see where they lead.

Lisa: When you go off on a tangent—that's when the magic happens in your artistic process!

Martha: Exactly.

Lisa: That's where the beautiful stuff happens. And the unexpected stuff, too.

Martha: Yeah, that's the thing I would tell people. Just embrace the tangents. Eventually, you'll understand how to harness them. But in the beginning, you just have to do it and then see what happens. Sometimes, your tangents fail. I've made some really stupid stuff. So that's another thing: don't be afraid of the stupid stuff that you make. It's part of it. The failure is part of it.

Lisa: The stuff that doesn't work is part of it.

Martha: Yeah, because it leads you to something else.

Lisa: That's right, or at least you know you'll never do *that* again.

Martha: Yeah. Or one little part of it will be like, "Oh my God, that's great," and then you just expand upon that and get rid of the glitter that didn't work.

GO OUTSIDE INTO THE WORLD AND BE MINDFUL OF WHAT YOU SEE

One of the best ways to find inspiration and discover new possibilities for things like subject matter, color, or pattern in your work is to go out into the world and pay attention. Most of the time when we're outside of our home or studio, our focus is on getting somewhere—to the grocery store, to pick up our kid at school, or to go to the post office to drop off packages. So while we might notice a few things that intrigue us, we typically don't actually see and absorb much because we're on a familiar route and we're simply processing our day or making a mental notice about what we have to do next.

Conversely, getting out into the world with the specific goal of paying attention always causes us to see things we wouldn't have otherwise noticed. We call this practicing mindfulness. Mindfulness happens when we intentionally focus on the present moment and are sensitive to our environment. When most people think of mindfulness, they think of the practice of sitting in silent meditation. Meditation is one mindfulness practice. But mindfulness doesn't just include sitting meditation. It can happen with your eyes wide open, and be part of your everyday active life at home, at work, and out in the world.

For example, almost every day I walk my dog, and I try to focus on using that time as an opportunity to take a look around and try to notice something new, instead of being absorbed in my thoughts or worries or obsessing over something annoying that happened earlier that day. I practice listening to sounds, looking up to the sky and down to the ground, and zooming in on things that I might not see otherwise. Contrary to popular belief, this kind of mindfulness doesn't require *not thinking*, but instead simply trains our minds to focus on what we see or hear around us in the present moment, instead of on thoughts about the past or future. Mindfulness actually leads to new ideas and divergent thinking! I sometimes get my best ideas when I am out on my daily walks. No doubt, the practice of paying attention can feel challenging, because obsessive thoughts want to take over. But with practice (just like anything!), mindfulness becomes easier and more fluid the more you do it.

FIND A SPACE TO BE ALONE TO CREATE

Many artists, even those who are extroverts, like to work alone. "The creative act is a process that often unfolds in solitary reflection," write Kaufman and Gregoire. "The trope of the reclusive writer and the introverted artist stems from a significant truth of creativity. In order to make art, we must find the space to become intimate with our own minds." In order for the creative process to expand, we get into our own worlds where there is less chance for interruption or the fear of judgment from others. Making sure that you have a space and blocks of time to be alone to create are important to your development. For some artists, being alone is a way of life, or it's already built into their routine. For example, I work from my studio, and I spend most of my time alone. I don't have children and my partner works in an office across town. But many artists either share studios with other artists or they work from home, with kids and partners. While working around other people is inevitable (and also beneficial at times), carving out time and space to create alone can help you focus and work without the distraction. Find and take advantage of times in the day when you can work alone.

FIND A FEEDBACK PARTNER OR FORM A CRITIQUE GROUP

Finding a space to work alone is essential to the development of your voice, but so is finding ways to engage with other people to talk about your work. One of the best ways you can bolster the development of your voice is to talk to other artists about your work and invite their feedback. In my early days as an artist, I shared a studio with my friend Jamie Vasta. Jamie is an accomplished artist with two prestigious art degrees. After sharing a studio together for a few months, Jamie and I began helping each other problem-solve issues in our work. At the time, I was painting portraits, and her perspective around what aspects of my portraits were off (it was usually the eyes!) was invaluable to me because I couldn't always see it. She'd say things like, "Maybe if you moved this eye slightly to the left." Jamie also began asking me to help her problem-solve her work. When she felt frustrated with an aspect of a painting, she asked me what I thought she should do to resolve it. We asked each other questions and helped each other work through issues on a regular basis. I realized over time, we'd formed our own little critique group. As someone who never went to art school and who didn't previously talk to people often about my work, discussing my work with Jamie was invaluable for me. I learned so much from her.

Likewise, when I signed with my former illustration agent Lilla, she began giving me feedback that proved transformative. She pointed out when I hadn't developed an illustration enough, or when something seemed sloppy or lacking an element that would make it more robust. She pushed me to add more detail and raise the complexity of my illustrations. Years later, I still think about feedback that both Jamie and Lilla offered about my work, both positive and critical.

Sometimes feedback can come, as it did for me, from one or two trusted mentors or fellow artists, but it can also come in a group environment. I know many artists who have either joined or formed groups of three or more people who meet regularly to offer each other feedback on things like composition, subject matter, messaging, and color in their work. Of course, you can take or leave whatever feedback you like (you are always the boss of your work). But fellow artists can also help you think about your work differently and assist you to work through quandaries or slumps with suggestions. When you form a feedback group, always start first by forging an environment of mutual respect through norms of healthy and considerate communication so that the sessions feel productive and don't leave you feeling worse about your work or without a sense of how to move forward.

TAKE CLASSES

Like joining a feedback group, taking classes, especially classes that stretch your skills or introduce you to new media, will almost always advance the development of your creative voice. Many artists and most colleges and community centers offer art classes to the general public. Some cities have workshop spaces dedicated to offering art and design classes. Conveniently, many classes are offered online. Sometimes classes serve the purpose of sharpening your skills in a particular area—drawing facial features or hand gestures, forming perfect bowls using a pottery wheel, or creating digital animation. But sometimes taking a class just for fun that doesn't necessarily have much to do with your artistic or professional goals is the best reason of all. Several years ago, I took an altered book class from book arts master Lisa Kokin. The class, which stretched over a couple of months, met in Lisa's large studio. We used discarded books as our substrate and constructed collages and sculptures made from bits of old books and magazines. While this class didn't lead me to a new career as a book artist, it did lead me to use book matter as collage elements in my work—a significant shift in my art practice. More importantly, the class gave me an opportunity to stop thinking about my own illustration projects for a few hours every week and focus on a divergent direction, for pure enjoyment. Just like getting outside and paying attention to our environment sparks creativity, the act of creating is in itself an act of mindfulness. Immersing ourselves in learning something new helps keep our brains stimulated, which supports the creative life cycle.

BRAINSTORM

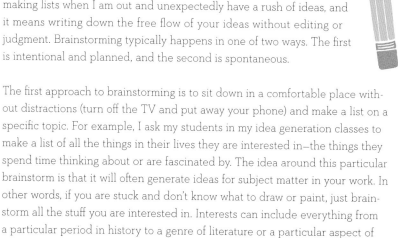

I sometimes teach a class for artists about generating ideas as part of developing your artistic voice. One of the main things I cover in the class is the power of brainstorming. You might remember from my story of the initially disastrous trip to the surface design trade show how much I love brainstorming and how helpful it can be, especially when you are stuck for ideas or inspiration. Brainstorming requires just two things: paper and a writing implement. You can also brainstorm lists on your phone or computer. I use my phone a lot for making lists when I am out and unexpectedly have a rush of ideas, and it means writing down the free flow of your ideas without editing or judgment. Brainstorming typically happens in one of two ways. The first is intentional and planned, and the second is spontaneous.

The first approach to brainstorming is to sit down in a comfortable place without distractions (turn off the TV and put away your phone) and make a list on a specific topic. For example, I ask my students in my idea generation classes to make a list of all the things in their lives they are interested in—the things they spend time thinking about or are fascinated by. The idea around this particular brainstorm is that it will often generate ideas for subject matter in your work. In other words, if you are stuck and don't know what to draw or paint, just brainstorm all the stuff you are interested in. Interests can include everything from a particular period in history to a genre of literature or a particular aspect of nature. Maybe you are fascinated by a form of pop culture, a genre of design, a country, a movement in fashion, a celebrity, an urban legend, a particular song. Your list of interests is as limitless as your interests! You can do an intentional, planned brainstorm around just about any topic and generate ideas for a body of work or for your next personal challenge. Or you can be more specific and brainstorm things that are related to your existing work, like new directions, tangents, and parallel themes.

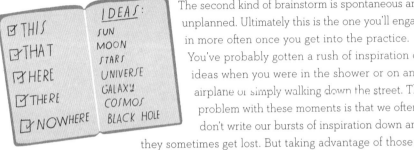

The second kind of brainstorm is spontaneous and unplanned. Ultimately this is the one you'll engage in more often once you get into the practice. You've probably gotten a rush of inspiration or ideas when you were in the shower or on an airplane or simply walking down the street. The problem with these moments is that we often don't write our bursts of inspiration down and they sometimes get lost. But taking advantage of those moments is where the amazing stuff begins. I keep a journal of lists (from my to-do lists to notes from meetings to brainstorm lists) that I try to carry with me everywhere (except maybe in the shower, of course). And then when I get an unexpected rush of ideas, I jot them down. When a journal feels too cumbersome to carry, I rely on the notes section of my phone. In both my journal and my phone, there are lists of words and phrases, ideas for new pieces, and things to research when I have time.

The essential part of brainstorming is to write down everything that comes into your mind without any filters, and not to break up the process with analysis about whether an idea will work or won't or whether something is a good idea or not. You can eventually narrow down your lists as a second step, or regroup items in a new list, but most brainstorms should be a free flow of ideas. Once you tell your brain, "Stop! That idea won't work," your brain will also begin to filter other potentially good ideas as bad ideas. Remember, it's just a list, not anything you have to act on right away. I go back and refer to my lists when I am feeling a lull of ideas or a creative block. I also add to them when new ideas arise!

DEVELOP YOUR VOCABULARY
AND BECOME AN EXPERT

One of my favorite pieces of advice in this book is from Sean Qualls. He reminds us that your voice becomes stronger when you "develop your vocabulary." Of course, he doesn't literally mean your vocabulary of words. He means your vocabulary of interests, knowledge, and ideas. We develop our vocabulary by going deep into learning and exploring the world—reading books and magazines, watching films, listening to podcasts, looking at art, traveling, and meeting new people. Through those experiences, you want to look for what speaks to you. Then, dive in and become an expert in those things that are inspiring or interesting. You might recall that Martha Rich goes deep into research about "weird" stuff that she becomes obsessed with (like church snake handlers), and much of that becomes the foundation for her subject matter. Become an expert by consuming knowledge, then expand your imagination and channel what you learn into your work as an artist.

GET OUT TO SUPPORT AND LEARN FROM
OTHER ARTISTS

Your journey as an artist will rest on the backs of other artists who have paved the way before you. Likewise, you will be paving the way for artists who come after you. Our ability to thrive creatively depends on the generosity we offer each other—in sharing knowledge and skills, resources and strategies. One of the best ways to benefit from what other artists have to offer you is getting out and supporting them. This means going to art openings, purchasing the work of artists when you are able, going to hear artists give talks, taking classes from artist who teach, and reading books by fellow artists. When you engage with other artists, you are not only supporting them, you are also learning about their work, their process, their inspiration, their struggles, their triumphs, their approaches for thriving in their careers. All of this knowledge and perspective will not only help you develop your own creative voice, it will also help you build a network of friends, mentors, and teachers who will support you over your entire journey as an artist.

STAY OPEN TO ALL EXPERIENCES

One of the key ingredients in stimulating creativity and in developing your artistic voice is what researchers Kaufman and Gregoire call "openness to experience." When we are open to experiencing and engaging with life fully, both the light and dark, and when we think in terms of possibility, even in challenging circumstances, our capacity for creative thinking is boundless. New experiences become the material integral to your artistic voice. Openness to experience is the "strongest and most consistent personality trait that predicts creative achievement." Openness is essential to creativity.

Openness to experience comes in many forms, from a desire for digging into and finding solutions to problems, to an active desire for learning, to having intense emotional reactions to music and art, and to being available to others and the depth of human emotion. When we engage in things that are new or uncomfortable, and we are open to those experiences, we experience creativity's rewards. Even simple things like taking a class to learn something new, walking a new route with the dog each day, listening to a different genre of music, or taking an illustration assignment that feels slightly outside your comfort zone can wake you up creatively.

"THINK LIKE A BEGINNER"

"In the beginner's mind there are many possibilities, but in the expert's there are few," wrote Zen master Suzuki Roshi. One of the best ways to stay open to experiences is to think like a beginner. When you adopt a beginner's mind, there are an unlimited number of possibilities available to you. Conversely, when you consider yourself educated and experienced (aka knowing everything), you see fewer possibilities. According to an article by researcher Victor Ottati and colleagues in *The Journal of Experimental Social Psychology*, approaching your work (and everything, really) with the mind of a beginner —even the stuff you're technically an expert at—will increase your ability to learn, grow skill, and activate more creative thinking. It will also open you up to different perspectives and possibilities. When you find yourself saying "That can't be done" or "I could never do that" or "That will never be successful," stop and allow yourself to open your mind to positive outcomes, including that while failure is an option, so is the fact that something might actually work! When you think like a beginner, you are taking in information during the day and listening without judgment in an attempt to learn something new. When you find yourself being curious about something, allow yourself to explore!

REMEMBER, YOU ARE THE BOSS OF YOUR WORK AND HOW YOU MAKE IT

One of the things that hinders artists the most is the fear of "doing it wrong." Regardless of what anyone has ever told you, one of the greatest things about being an artist is that *there is no "right" or "wrong" way to make anything.* Sure, in some cases, some techniques are speedier and sometimes clients prefer things submitted in a certain format. Depending on your professional goals, you should pay attention to those kinds of guidelines. But for the most part, you get to invent your own process and your own set of rules for how you use your media and what you create, even if it means throwing away everything you ever learned in art school and making things up as you go. Giving yourself permission to do things in the way that works for you will not only keep you more engaged in the creative process, but making your own rules will help your work to stand out as different. Experiment, find the ways you like to work, open yourself to new solutions, and then own those approaches as your very own process.

NOW IT'S YOUR TURN

"Every artist was first an amateur," wrote Ralph Waldo Emerson. I remember hearing this quote for the first time early in my creative path and being filled with enormous relief. It was a reminder that even my greatest heroes—the ones whose work I idolized for years—were once novices too. Often, when we watch other artists from afar, we make the faulty assumption that they've been as skilled and as prolific and as talented since the day they began making art. In ninety nine percent of the cases, save for a few prodigies, that's almost never true. The vast majority of artists, even your heroes, were once total beginners, made bad artwork, struggled with technical skills, blundered, felt lost, and questioned their work. Even as experienced artists with fully formed voices, your heroes still struggle. They still face learning curves, make mistakes, feel fear, and sometimes don't know where they are headed next.

This truth is one of the most important things to remember as you work to develop your own voice as an artist. Developing an artistic voice is not a miraculous process reserved only for a few innately talented people. Every single person who chooses to embark on a creative path has to work at it. The unfolding of your voice requires showing up and working hard. It requires being willing to create failures, to ask for feedback, and to go back and try all over again. It requires staying open. It requires moving outside what's comfortable and being vulnerable. Sure, that might feel daunting, but the good news is that if you are willing to do that work, you *will* develop your artistic voice. And if you commit to working your magic, it will lead to extraordinary things—works of art that transform lives, disrupt the status quo, change the conversation, shift mindsets, lift spirits, and offer comfort or connection to people who need it most. Are you ready?

BIBLIOGRAPHY

Atwood, Margaret. *Moral Disorder and Other Stories*. New York: Anchor Books, 2008.

Dostoyevsky, Fyodor. *White Knights and Other Stories*. New York: Dover Thrift Editions, 2008.

Eliot, T. S. *The Sacred Wood: Essays on Poetry and Criticism*. New York: Alfred A. Knopf, 1921.

Emerson, Ralph Waldo. "Progress of Culture." In *The Collected Works of Ralph Waldo Emerson, Volume VIII: Letters and Social Aims*, edited by Ronald A. Bosco, Glen M. Johnson, and Joel Myerson. Cambridge, MA: Belknap Press of Harvard University Press, 2010.

Glass, Ira. "Ira Glass on Story Telling." *This American Life*, August 18, 2009. https://www.thisamericanlife.org/extras/ira-glass-on-storytelling.

Jong, Erika. *Conversations with Erica Jong*. Jackson: University Press of Mississippi, 2002.

Kaufman, Scott Barry, and Carolyn Gregoire. *Wired to Create*. New York: TarcherPerigee, 2016.

Kleon, Austin. *Steal Like an Artist*. New York: Workman Publishing, 2012.

Ottati, Victor, Erika D. Price, Chase Wilson, and Nathanael Sumaktoyo. "When Self-Perceptions of Expertise Increase Closed-Minded Cognition: The Dogmatism Effect." *The Journal of Experimental Social Psychology* 61 (November 2015): 131–138.

Roshi, Suzuki. *Zen Mind, Beginner's Mind: Informal Talks on Zen Meditation and Practice*. Boulder, CO: Shambhala Publications, 2011.

Rubin, Gretchen. "Harnessing the Power of Frequency." In *Manage Your Day to Day: Build Your Routine, Find Your Focus, and Sharpen Your Creative Mind*, edited by Jocelyn K. Glei (99U Book Series). Seattle: Amazon Publishing, 2013.

Shahn, Ben. *The Shape of Content*. Cambridge, MA: Harvard University Press, 1958.

ACKNOWLEDGMENTS

First and foremost, thank you to my longtime editor, Bridget Watson Payne, for suggesting that a short blog post I wrote on the topic of finding your voice could expand into a book of 30,000 words. Thank you also to my talented book designer, Kristen Hewitt, and everyone at Chronicle Books for continuing to give my work a beautiful platform over the past decade. This book would not exist without you and your confidence in me! Special thanks to my literary agent, Stefanie Von Borstel, my beloved advocate and navigator. Most important, thank you to all of the fellow artists, confidants, curators, and mentors who have inspired me, encouraged me, and supported me in my journey to find my own voice over the past twelve years. This list includes, but is not limited to: Lilla Rogers, Elizabeth Gilbert, Debbie Millman, Jamie Vasta, Lorena Siminovich, Courtney Cerruti, Janine Vangool, Sara Jensen, Danielle Krysa, Lisa Solomon, Eric Rewitzer, Annie Galvin, Jen Hewett, Tiffany Han, Amy Rowan, Emily McDowell, Margo Tantau, Sara Stevenson, Anne Weill, Victor Maldonado, Anna Joyce, Diana Fayt, Mati McDonough, Anna Dorfman, Troy Litten, Jennifer Orkin Lewis, Brett Stenson, Tuesday Bassen, Kristine Kinoko Evans, Faythe Levine, Kate Bingaman-Burt, Claudia Pearson, Katharine Dougherty, Carol Henke, Wendy MacNaughton, Jason Sturgill, Andy Miller, Lindsay Stripling, Trish Grantham, Rena Tom, Brené Brown, Vonn Sumner, Christopher Dibble, Dawline-Jane Oni-Eseleh, Grace Bonney, George McCalman, Meg Mateo Ilasco, Yvonne Perez Emerson, Rachel Frankel, Veronica Corzo-Duchardt, Yao Cheng, Heather Posten, Trina Turk, Jen Bekman, and Stephanie Chefas. And to my mom, Gerrie Congdon, and my sister, Stephanie Congdon Barnes. You are all a part of me forever.

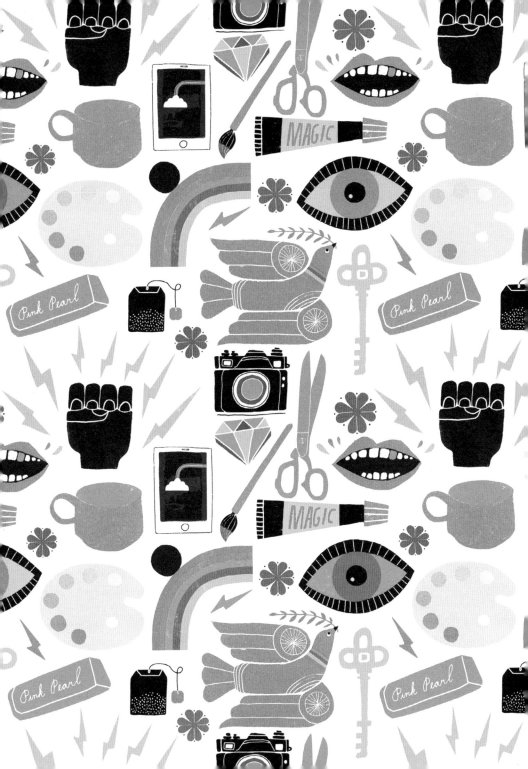